The
Media-Savvy
Student

Teaching Media Literacy Skills

Guofang Wan AND **Hong Cheng**

Zephyr Press

Chicago

The Media-Savvy Student
Teaching Media Literacy Skills
Grades 2-6
©2004 by Guofang Wan and Hong Cheng
Printed in the United States of America
ISBN: 1-56976-170-1
Editing: Melanie Mallon
Interior Design: Rattray Design
Illustrations: Laura D'Argo
Cover: Rattray Design

Published by:
Zephyr Press
An imprint of Chicago Review Press
814 North Franklin Street
Chicago, Illinois 60610
www.zephyrpress.com

The Internet is an open and rapidly changing system; Web sites may contain material
inappropriate for children. Best educational practice indicates that an adult should preview all Web sites before sending students to visit them.

Contents

4 Internet-Savvy Kids 115

Acknowledgments

We want to acknowledge the pioneers of media literacy education and the children who use mass media daily, both nationally and internationally. It is they who have stimulated our interest in and passion for media literacy education.

We have had a great experience working with the publishing team at Zephyr Press, without which this book would be impossible. We want to thank Ms. Jenny Flynn, who believed in the value of this book and encouraged us to engage in it.

We appreciate Ms. Libby Birky's efforts in making the book lively and appealing to readers by providing reference illustrations.

We are also very thankful to our family members and friends who were supportive and understanding during the days and nights we worked on the book. Our special appreciation goes to Melissa, our ten-year-old daughter, who provides us with daily chances to observe a child's use of mass media and chances for media literacy education at home. Her comments and suggestions from a child's point of view add greatly to the book.

This book is the fruit of the joint efforts of everyone mentioned above. Please accept our heartfelt thanks to all of you.

Introduction to Media Literacy

"It is no longer enough simply to read and write. Students must also become literate in the understanding of visual images. Our children must learn how to spot a stereotype, isolate a social cliché, and distinguish facts from propaganda, analysis from banter, and important news from coverage."

—Ernest Boyer

Welcome to the world of media literacy. If you are an elementary classroom teacher, this book is designed specifically to help you meet educational goals for media literacy and to explore the field of media literacy with your students. *The Media-Savvy Student* provides you with both theory and practice of media literacy. This introduction discusses what media literacy is, why it is important for children so young to know, and how to integrate it into your existing curriculum. The chapters that follow introduce you to a selection of meaningful and interesting ideas and resources through 20 thematic units that enable you to teach media literacy in your classroom. Actively engaging students in analyzing and creating media messages, media literacy reflects curriculum integration, student-centered teaching, inquiry-based education, problem solving in cooperative learning, and alternatives to standardized testing.

What Is Media Literacy?

In North America, most media literacy organizations and experts will agree with this description of media literacy: the ability to access, analyze, evaluate, and communicate information in a variety of formats, including print and nonprint. Nonprint media include television, video and audio recordings, electronic games, films, photography, and the Internet.

Other explanations of media literacy add to our definition. Shepherd (1993) defined media literacy as an informed and critical understanding of mass media that results from an examination of the techniques, technologies, and institutions that are involved in media production; the ability to critically analyze media messages; and the recognition of the role that audiences play in making meaning from those messages.

Media literacy also refers to the understanding of media and the use of it as a source of information, entertainment, enrichment, growth, empowerment, and communication. Equally important to understanding the media is to learn how to use technology rather than letting technology use you (Sutton 1993).

Duncan et al. (1989) defined media literacy specifically for school settings as "helping students develop an informed and critical understanding of the nature of mass media, the techniques used by them, and the impact of those techniques. More specifically, media literacy aims to increase students' understanding and enjoyment of how the media work, how they produce meaning, how they are organized, and how they construct reality. Media literacy also aims to provide students with the ability to create media products" (7).

In this book we will look at media literacy as an informed and critical understanding of the mass media, and as the ability to do the following.

Access information: This refers to skills such as reading, locating, selecting, and organizing information from a variety of sources, such as print, video, and the Internet.

Analyze information: This refers to analyzing and exploring how messages are constructed. Analysis requires skills such as making effective use of knowledge, determining the genre of a work, making inferences about cause and effect, identifying the author's purpose, and recognizing social, political, historical, and aesthetic contexts of information.

Evaluate information: This refers to evaluating media messages using one's own ethical, moral, and democratic principles. It includes skills such as judging the usefulness of a message, using prior knowledge to interpret a work, identifying values in a message, and appreciating the aesthetic quality of a work.

Communicate information: This refers to expressing or creating one's own messages using a variety of media tools. It includes reading, writing, speaking, understanding audience, using symbols to convey meaning, organizing ideas, and capturing the attention of an audience. It also calls for skills such as editing, revising, and creating messages with multimedia tools.

We believe media-literate people are better citizens because they understand that television is made to convey ideas, information, and news from someone else's perspective; they understand that media use specific techniques to create emotional effects; they are aware that all media benefit some people and leave others out; they can pose and answer questions about who the beneficiaries are and who is left out and why; they use alternative sources of information and entertainment; and they use television for their own advantage and enjoyment (Kipping cited in Media Awareness Network 2002b).

Why Teach Media Literacy to Children?

Duncan et al. (1989) argues that media dominate our political and cultural lives; almost all information beyond our direct experience comes to us through media; media are powerful shapers of values and behaviors; media literacy can increase our appreciation of media products; and media literacy can make us active media users.

In our view, traditional literacy (reading and writing) alone is far from enough for our students to be successful in the 21st century. Becoming literate in the new century means that students also need to understand the influence of media on our society, develop strategies to critically analyze media, and become independent from the influence of media. It is important, therefore, that beginning in the primary grades, children acquire this empowering life skill by learning to use media resources critically and thoughtfully.

In the United States and around the world, the ways people access entertainment, obtain information, and interact with each other are changing rapidly, challenging us as individuals and as a society. We as a society are becoming more and more dependent on electronic media for information, entertainment, and communication. We turn on our TV for the latest happenings in the world, put on our CD Walkman when we go out to jog, read online newspapers, and keep in touch with our relatives on the other side of the earth through e-mail and cellular phones. Most of the information and resources we need are online, and thousands of products and services are there, too. The Internet has hit the road in several car models. Through voice-activated technology, you can talk to your car and it talks back to you (Naughton and Halpert 2001). Children turn on their favorite early morning cartoon shows to accompany their cereal, search the Internet for ocean animal projects, and entertain themselves during family trips in minivans that are equipped with DVD players and Nintendo. Families watch movies on DVD in the living room as a Friday night get-together. When we receive most of our information and entertainment from electronic media—such as television and the Internet—not from books, we certainly need a wider definition of literacy.

American children grow up surrounded by media: The average child's home contains three TVs, three radios, three tape players, two VCRs, two CD players, one video game player, and one computer (Diaz 1999). Children's bedrooms are rapidly becoming wired. Wireless Internet on handhelds and cellular phones will soon become a favorite. Electronic media take our children across the globe before we let them go across the street. Children between the ages of two and five watch an average of 31 hours of television per week. By the time a student finishes high school, he or she will have spent an average of 11,000 hours in school but 15,000 hours watching television (Cox 1996). This situation obviously calls for media literacy education in the classroom.

Virtually all that we know about the world beyond our immediate experience comes to us through media such as TV, radio, and the Internet. Media bring the world into our homes. From them, we learn about war and peace, the environment, new scientific discoveries, and so on. We are dependent upon mass communication for knowing what is going on in our physical, social, economic, and political environments. We also rely on media for entertainment and pleasure. Television, movies, and the Internet tell us how the world works, how to buy products, and how to behave toward others. The various powerful forms of electronic media that have appeared during the 20th century can benefit or harm children and communities depending on how they are used. Smart use of media can provide us with knowledge and skills, as well as entertainment. However, unwise use can be harmful to children in many ways.

Our heavy dependency on media would not be a problem if the media simply reflected reality. But each medium shapes reality in different ways, and we can no longer consider any message in any medium to be neutral or value free. All the messages that we come in contact with contain information about values, beliefs, and behaviors and are shaped by economic factors (Ontario Ministry of Education 1989). Digital technology and virtual reality can create any images and make anything look true to life. What seems to be real to our eyes may not be.

All news reports are carefully selected, reported, and edited by news providers. Often information about the world comes to us with built-in attitudes, interpretations, and values from media creators. These creators show us a selected and often unrepresentative view of the world. An interesting example is the diverse and conflicting reports given by the coalition and by the former Iraqi government about the United States-led war in Iraq. While the United States claimed its troops were deep into Baghdad, the Iraqi Information Minister denied it and said, "We are firmly in control of Baghdad." Audiences need to find out what is true by themselves. What is more, to make money, media sometimes provide us with sensational, shocking, or bizarre news and stories that distort our sense of reality. Our children should be encouraged to use media more critically and become mature media consumers. Media literacy is an alternative to censorship, boycotting, and blaming media.

Media Literacy Education in the United States

Many people are surprised to learn that for years, media literacy has been an established part of the educational system in Europe and other English-speaking countries, including Great Britain, Canada, and Australia. Government schools (K-12) in Canada devote one fourth of English syllabuses to media study (Brown 2001). In Great Britain, as well as in Canada, Australia, and Spain, media literacy is required as part of the language arts program in grades 7 through 12 (Hobbs 1997). The United States has lagged behind countries such as Canada, Australia, Chile, India, Great Britain, France, and Jordan in media education.

Since the early 1990s, however, support groups like the Center for Media Education, the Center for Media Literacy, the National Telemedia Council, Citizens for Media Literacy, and the Children's Media Policy Network have been created to educate the American public about the need for media education. In 1998 the National Communication Association developed standards for media literacy in K-12 education (National Communication Association 1998).

Kubey and Baker (1999) reported on the new and hopeful development of media literacy education in the United States. They examined current educational frameworks in the states and found that at least 48 state curricular frameworks contained one or more elements calling for some form of media education. They found that media education appeared in the following curriculum categories: 1) English, language, and communication arts—46 states; 2) social studies, history, and civics—30 states; 3) health, nutrition, and consumerism—30 states; and 4) media strand—7 states. You can find out where media literacy stands in your home state standards by checking Kubey and Baker's article or consulting the standards-related Web resources provided on page 158.

Baran and Davis (2003) reported that "thirty-four states now mandate media literacy in their primary and secondary school curricula" (377). This indicates that the media literacy movement is gaining momentum in the American academic community and that U.S. educators have begun to recognize the value of media literacy education. Although many teachers and administrators believe that media education is important, putting it into practice is still not easy. The lack of time, materials, and teacher training are among the major barriers. Although media literacy is called for in some form in 48 states, it is not delivered as widely as it is mandated.

Media literacy education in the United States is heavily influenced by the theory and practice established in Canada, Great Britain, and Australia. In the 1970s media literacy in the United States emphasized protecting children from negative effects and questionable values disseminated through mass media. The purpose was to guide students to be selective in program choices and to understand the underlying determinants of media presentations and commercial advertising. Media education relied mainly on parents at home. In the 1980s progress in media literacy education slowed down in the United States. Over the past decade there has been a shift toward an emphasis on media literacy as empowerment—stressing critical-thinking and production skills. Media literacy education now shows students the factors behind media operations and media aesthetics so that they can make sense out of media products and assess the value as well as the weaknesses of these products. More media literacy materials are now aimed at schools and teachers. A further goal of media literacy today is to help students appreciate their own culture and that of others—including social, political, and economic aspects—through media exposure.

What Media Literacy Skills Should We Teach Children?

We believe that it is crucial for elementary children to learn about the following aspects of media culture.

We Make Meaning

We are active media users. We support, question, and challenge what we see, read, and hear. For example, when we watch TV, we try to connect what we see with everything else we know already. We get involved in TV programs with different levels of understanding because of who we are and what life experiences we bring to our TV viewing. Thus we can filter and change what TV presents by the way we watch it. It is very important to talk back to programs and news reports when you do not agree with them.

Media Literacy Principles

The principles of media literacy that are commonly explored by various curriculum writers in Great Britain, Canada, Australia, and the United States include the following.

Media are constructions: Media do not present simple reflections of reality. All messages are carefully selected, edited, and designed by media. Seeing is not believing in the world of virtual reality. Media show us a selected and often unrepresentative view of the world that often seems to be true. We need to learn to tell reality from representations of reality.

Media representations construct reality: The way the world is presented by the media affects and influences the way we perceive the world. Because most of our experiences of the world come directly from the media with built-in attitudes, interpretations, and conclusions, media, to a great extent, give us our sense of reality.

Audiences negotiate their own meanings: Audiences are not passive recipients of media messages; rather, they filter media messages through their own beliefs, value systems, and prior knowledge. People with differing ethnic backgrounds may come up with different perceptions, perspectives, and feelings about the same program.

Media constructions have commercial purposes: Real understanding of media content cannot be separated from the financial factors that drive the media industry. Media production is a business and needs to make a profit. It gives the public what they want in order to make money.

Media messages contain values and ideologies: Media products are advertisements for values or ways of life for an existing social system. In American media, we might find values such as "consumption is the route to happiness" or ideas about the "proper" role of women.

Media have social and political consequences: Media have a wide range of social and political effects. Television, for example, can help to elect or impeach a president on the basis of image. This principle explores the way the media show, shape, reflect, and reinforce reality. It involves understanding who and what is portrayed and how, as well as which groups and individuals in our society are left out of the picture.

Each medium has unique characteristics: A medium explores the relationship between form and content. The understanding of particular characteristics of each medium illustrates to us the reasons why the same event reported by different media creates different impressions and different messages. It enables us to see not only what we are told, but how.

The Media World Is Not Always Real

Media makers, photographers, writers, and editors select pictures, stories, and news reports for us. We get to see, read, and hear only what they present to us. Like storytellers, they have many ways to create images and illusions to keep their audience interested and involved. Sometimes they present a perfect fantasy world to us, and sometimes they present a horrible, devastating, or violent world to us. The world created by media is not always real. Comparing the same news story reported by two sources with different perspectives reveals how different this presented world can be.

Media Use Special Techniques

Media makers use techniques to achieve special effects. We can identify the camera angles, music, special effects, and symbols that make scary scenes more scary, tyrants more evil, or advertised candies sweeter. Some examples of these techniques are close-ups, fade-outs, music changes, and use of color. Knowing these techniques helps us appreciate them and makes us less susceptible to media manipulation.

Media Carry Ideologies and Bias

Through media we can see producers' viewpoints, what they like and what they do not, and who or what they regard as important. We should expect subjectivity and biases in media, and learn to challenge them. Some people are shown as victims and some as heroes. Some are glamorized and some are despised. Some information makes headlines and other information is left out. Children should learn to think critically and ask questions such as "Who benefits?" "Who loses?" "What is the viewpoint of the report?" and "What is the purpose of the program?" This is important citizenship training in a democratic society.

Media are Moneymaking Businesses

There is no free lunch in the media world. Media are moneymaking networks. Producers sell programs to networks. Networks sell time to advertisers. Advertisers sell products to viewers. By watching the programs, we are exposed to commercials urging us to buy. Children should learn to resist the temptations of materialism from media. It is important to know that media owners, production costs, and advertisers play important roles in gatekeeping for media production (Media Awareness Network 2003).

How Do We Integrate Media Literacy into Existing Curriculum?

Many classroom teachers may ask, "How can I add media literacy to my already crowded curriculum?" The answer is that media literacy can be easily integrated into your existing curriculum at all grade levels because by nature, media literacy encourages an interdisciplinary approach to education; it is not a new subject to add to the school day. Rather, media literacy is a set of skills that can be learned through other subjects and content areas. Media literacy–like traditional literacy–is a part of every subject. Just as reading and writing are required in science, math, and social studies as well as in English courses, so is media literacy. Media education is relevant to science, math, social studies, the visual and performing arts as well as language arts. Teachers can make connections across content areas by teaching with media and about media. Media literacy creates an authentic learning environment for students by providing meaningful and relevant tasks. The following examples demonstrate how media literacy is part of every subject you already teach.

Media literacy supports traditional literacy because both involve reading and writing for the same purposes. With traditional literacy, we read to receive and comprehend information and write to express, entertain, inform, and convince; with media literacy, we view and read to receive and comprehend information and compose to express, entertain, inform, and convince. For example, when we ask students to compare the novel and movie versions of the Harry Potter series, we teach critical-reading skills, comparison, comprehension, drawing conclusions, decoding, and logical reasoning skills at the same time. When students make posters of TV viewing rules, they practice writing skills and using art to convey meaning.

Media provide us with many wonderful opportunities for math education. The weather report tells us there is a 50 percent chance for rain; the morning newspaper reports the stock market numbers and gives us sports statistics. Think about the statistics, TV ratings, annual reports, opinion polls, daily weather reports, and weekend grocery sales in media and consider how many problem-solving math questions you can make each day out of the examples in media. We can also teach graphical displays using bar or pie graphs in newspapers and magazines as real examples. When one brand of cereal makes the claim on TV that three out of the four interviewed children love it, we can ask children, "What about the thousands of other children not surveyed?"

Science is a natural part of media literacy. Various scientific studies and topics are reported in media, such as on the Discovery Channel, every day. The reports in media about the SARS (severe acute respiratory syndrome) epidemic presented a great chance to discuss the spread of infectious diseases and show students that human beings still have a lot to discover and study. Science fiction movies such as *Contact*, *Deep Impact*, and *Armageddon* are intriguing to our students. Teachers can take advantage of students' interest in these movies and explore the scientific principles depicted. The studies of inventions of media, such as TV, the Internet, paper, and printing are great science topics to cover in elementary curriculum.

Social studies curriculum is closely related to media literacy as well. Media literacy reinforces multicultural education and promotes cultural pluralism. It encourages students to consider multiple perspectives on current and historical multicultural issues. It also involves analyzing and evaluating how media represent different social groups, cultures, and ideologies. For example, when we teach students how to identify ethnic stereotypes from TV images, a social study topic is involved. The use of e-mail greeting cards can take our students on virtual trips to celebrate holidays native to many other countries in the world. Thus we can teach geography, such as countries and continents, as well as world cultures at the same time. World history and American history can be taught during discussions of current world affairs depicted in media.

Studies on resources, the environment, and human populations can be integrated in the discussion of commercialism and materialism. Reports on the conservation of rainforest resources can lead to the understanding of the few remaining nomadic tribes on earth.

Health and physical education can be addressed as well with media literacy. Students' understanding of safety is enhanced while learning about Internet safety rules. Personal health is a natural extension of discussion about ads for healthy snacks, exercise machines, dental care products, and tobacco and alcohol. Discussion of nutrition we receive from good food can lead to discussion of how the body uses food and to recommendations for eating a variety of foods, less sugar, less fat, and to leading a tobacco- and alcohol-free life. Reading news about the outbreak of SARS can be a great way to address personal hygiene, such as washing hands before meals.

Art education and media literacy go hand in hand. What techniques are used to attract our attention in a TV program or newspaper ad? How does digital technology create virtual reality? How are TV programs made using camera techniques? Knowledge of art helps answer these questions. Techniques, styles, and media of art can be taught with various media literacy units when illustrations of books, objects, and projects are required.

We empower students by nurturing their higher-order thinking skills. This goal of education is supported by media literacy because teaching students how to use critical-thinking skills to understand, analyze, and evaluate media, and to make smart choices, is a major purpose of media education. For example, when teaching persuasive techniques used in commercials, students learn how to assess their own needs against the urge to buy. Students use critical-thinking skills to judge whether or not the information they find online is accurate.

Media literacy offers teachers opportunities to develop various teaching strategies to meet students' needs and the requirements of different learning styles. For example, showing a video about rainforests as an introduction to a rainforest unit will catch everybody's attention and make the topic more accessible to students who have never been to a rainforest. Visual and auditory learners respond much better to visual and audio teaching materials. So students may learn more effectively in the classroom through multimedia means.

Media literacy provides teachers with authentic tasks and materials to motivate communication and language-learning among students who are learning English as a second language. Through TV commercials, menus, hotel receipts, children's books, newspapers, and the Internet, ESL children will be exposed to authentic and contemporary English. Materials beyond textbooks such as drama, songs, objects, and audiovisual materials help ESL students to learn more effectively.

About This Book

The purposes we had in mind when we created this book were 1) to provide elementary teachers of grades 2-6 with intriguing materials that they can integrate in their everyday teaching to meet state goals of media literacy; 2) to introduce the concept of media literacy and the importance of teaching media literacy in elementary classrooms; 3) to provide teachers with a media literacy curriculum and with practical ideas and ready-made materials to teach media literacy in their classrooms; and 4) to help students understand the influence of media on their lives, develop strategies to critically analyze media, and become mature media consumers. This book focuses primarily on electronic media, such as TV and the Internet, because children of this age group are heavy users of them.

We take a discovery and inquiry approach toward teaching and learning about media literacy. Students discover the truth or knowledge on their own instead of receiving it from the teacher through a prepackaged format. This approach helps students bring a part of themselves to the learning process and makes learning relevant to their lives. Learning takes place when students actively engage themselves in problem solving, decision making, logical thinking and reasoning, scientific inquiry, and collaboration with others. Teachers are facilitators of discussion, reading, writing, viewing, speaking, creating, and other learning activities.

The four chapters that follow contain 20 thematic units. Each chapter focuses on one major area of media literacy: mass media in general, television, advertising, and the Internet. The resources and bibliography contain valuable books, articles, and Websites with information on media literacy for teachers.

Chapter 1, Mass Media in Our Lives, consists of six units that provide students with an understanding of what mass media are, how pervasive they are in our lives, how we interact with them, and the characteristics of TV, the Internet, newspapers, and digital images. These units help students recognize their own media use habits and learn to take charge of their lives.

Chapter 2, Becoming Critical Viewers, covers the role viewing plays and its impact on our lives. All five units in this chapter work together to show children how to analyze programs and become more sophisticated critics. The thematic units teach children how to distinguish fantasy from reality, identify stereotypes, talk back to the TV, recognize the ways in which TV constructs reality, and understand why people interpret the same program differently.

Chapter 3, Advertising Is Everywhere, consists of four units designed to help children understand the nature and goals of advertising, to develop critical-thinking skills, to understand and identify advertising techniques, to take action in response to advertising, to assess needs against wants, and to realize that consumerism is not the only way to happiness. Through these unit activities, children become mature and informed consumers and citizens.

Chapter 4, Internet-Savvy Kids, introduces the Internet world to young children and helps them develop critical surfing skills so that they can safely and reliably use the Internet as a tool for lifelong learning. The units suggest ways to educate children about the benefits and risks involved in an online search; the basic open and nonprivate nature of the Internet; and ways to recognize bias, protect themselves from online marketing, protect their personal privacy, learn proper Internet behaviors, search for quality information, and learn about other countries through online greeting cards.

Each thematic unit includes the following components.

Rationale: An explanation of why it is important to teach the specific skills in the unit, particularly toward the goal of teaching media literacy.

Objectives: Specific objectives students will achieve.

Related Content Areas: The additional content areas the unit addresses, in conjunction with media literacy content. The content areas are based on the learning goals developed by professional education associations and organizations as guidelines (National Communication Association 1998; National Council of Teachers of English and International Reading Association 1996; National Council for the Social Studies 1994; National Research Council 1996; National Council of Teachers of Mathematics 2000; National Association for Sport and Physical Education 1995; Consortium of National Arts Education Associations 1994; and Joint Committee on National Health Education Standards 1995). Major content areas we outline include language arts, math, social studies, science, health and physical education, and fine arts. Language arts include reading, writing, speaking, listening, and research. Knowledge of technology is classified under media literacy, which is discussed as a content area in the Rationale and Objectives sections. History, geography, civics and government, and economics are included in social studies. Fine arts include drawing, music, dance, and theatre. Teachers will be able to translate these related content areas into their own state learning standards easily.

Preparation and Materials: A list of all preparation and materials required to make the unit successful. Some units require use of a computer and other equipment. These units can always be adapted to your classroom computer, software, and equipment access. We provide suggestions for doing so where relevant. We also provide an estimate of time required to complete the unit.

Procedure: Step-by-step instructions for teaching the activities of the unit.

Adaptations: Ways to adapt the activities for the specific needs of lower or upper elementary students and middle school students, gifted students, and those with special needs.

Assessments: Ideas for how to evaluate student understanding and learning through the unit activities. The assessments suggested are in various formats, including authentic assessment and paper-and-pencil assessment. The assessments include pretests, posttests, observations, projects, participation in discussions and activities, and so forth.

Handouts and informational sheets: Ready-made materials for teachers to use in the classroom, such as reproducible copies of concepts, definitions of terms, worksheets (with answer keys, starting on page 151), discussion guides, samples of classroom projects, and so forth. At your discretion, the handouts for students may be used instead as guides for you to teach from and facilitate discussion if the ideas and reading level are too complex for your particular students.

Some units require more time than others to complete. The duration of time needed for the completion of each thematic unit ranges anywhere from a few hours to two weeks, depending on the level of interest and commitment to the topics, and on the learning levels of your students. However, for each unit an estimated time is given for you to use as a guideline.

Some of us are further along the way than others in the journey toward media literacy, and this book starts at the beginning of the journey. We invite you to seek out the parts of the book that are most appropriate for you and your students. The book can be used in many ways. Some teachers may use several chapters, or parts of each chapter, while others use the entire book. Some teachers may choose to teach the Internet topics first, while others decide to teach television topics first. Each unit stands on its own, so feel free to start with the units that best fit your students' age, reading level, experience with media, and background. You may also choose to adapt lessons to fit your students' special needs. However you decide to use the book, we hope you enjoy the journey to media literacy education as much as we have. Bon voyage!

Mass Media in Our Lives

> ### In this chapter:
>
> **Unit 1:** *Let's Look at Mass Media*
>
> **Unit 2:** *What Goes on Behind the Scenes?*
>
> **Unit 3:** *What's the Net?*
>
> **Unit 4:** *What's in a Newspaper?*
>
> **Unit 5:** *Images in a Digital Age*
>
> **Unit 6:** *Media Culture Through the Eyes of Alien Friends*

Children are immersed daily in mass media images and messages. Some teach them about the world and entertain them, while others sell them ideas and promote deceptive, partial, stereotypical, and sometimes harmful perceptions. The purpose of the units in this chapter is to provide students with an understanding of what mass media are, what impact they have on our lives, how we interact with them, and the characteristics of TV, the Internet, newspapers, and digital images. These units also help students to recognize their own media use habits and learn to take charge of their lives.

Let's Look at Mass Media

Rationale

To learn the skills of media literacy, students need some background knowledge of mass media. This unit provides students with a basic understanding of mass media, including the definition of mass media, characteristics of several major media, and the major functions of mass media.

Objectives

- Students will be able to define mass media.
- Students will be able to name several examples of mass media.
- Students will be able to identify functions and features of mass media.

Related Content Areas

- **Language arts:** Students will use vocabulary in discussions and oral presentations; write descriptions; and use critical analysis, evaluation, and comparison.
- **Fine arts:** Students will demonstrate knowledge and understanding through performance.

Preparation and Materials

- Gather at least four samples of mass media, such as a TV, a VCR and videotape, a DVD player and DVD, a video game console, a computer, a record player and record, newspapers, magazines, a CD player and CD, or a radio.
- Make sure all students have paper and pencils or pens.
- Make copies for each student of the Getting to Know Mass Media handout (page 21).
- Estimated time for unit: 3 hours.

Procedure

1. As an introduction, ask students: "What is your favorite pastime?" List students' answers on the board. When students mention TV, CDs, movies, video games, or other mass media, explain that you will talk about some of their favorite pastimes today. Ask student volunteers to turn on the TV, radio, CD player, and whatever items you have on display, and then turn them off after a while.

2. Ask the class "What do you call these things we have on display?" Students may start to call out answers. Accept any reasonable answers.

3. Write both the singular form–"medium"–and the plural form–"media"–on the board and ask students to explain the difference or to look up both words in the dictionary to learn the difference. Explain that the displays are samples of various mass media.

> ➤ **TIP**
>
> *Consider having students bring in their favorite movies, video games, and CDs to make the unit even more relevant to them.*

4. Ask students to get into small groups. Each group picks one medium from the display. In small groups, students examine the chosen medium carefully and discuss the functions and features of it, recording their answers on a piece of paper. These discussion questions may help students get started:

   - What do you use this medium for?
   - What's special about your medium?
   - Who makes the medium and for whom?

5. On the board, list various media (see Various Mass Media, below, as a guide), then have students share the results of their discussions on chosen media. Facilitate the discussion and write down students' answers. Together look at the media list on the board and discuss similarities and unique features of various mass media. Conclude that each mass medium has something in common with the others—to inform, influence, entertain, and sell products to everyone in society—but each one also has its own particular characteristics.

Various Mass Media (with possible answers)

Types of Mass Media	Functions	Features	Sources and Audience
TV	Informs, sells, entertains, influences	Up-to-the-minute, live (sometimes), sound, portable (sometimes), color images, many channels, electronic	By a few for everyone
Radio	Informs, sells, entertains, influences	Up-to-the-minute, live, sound, portable, many stations, electronic	By a few for everyone
VCR and DVD player/burner	Records, informs, entertains, sells, influences	Recording and playback capabilities, sound, images, electronic	By a few for everyone
CD player/burner	Records, informs, entertains, sells, influences	Recording (sometimes) and playback capabilities, sound (especially music), portable (often), electronic	By a few for everyone
Video game console	Entertains, sells	Special sound and image effects, interactive, playback capabilities, electronic	By a few for everyone
Movie (in the theater)	Informs, sells, entertains, influences	Special sound and image effects, electronic, color, large screen	By a few for everyone
Magazine	Informs, sells, entertains, influences	Color images, words, rereadable, elaborated story, portable, print	By a few for everyone
Newspaper	Informs, sells, entertains, influences	Images, words, rereadable, brief stories, portable, print	By a few for everyone
Computer/Internet	Informs, sells, entertains and educates ("edutainment"), influences	Sound, images, words, interactive, huge amount of information, electronic	By a few for everyone

6. Together discuss "What are mass media?" The previous discussion of media similarities and differences should lead to the understanding that mass media are ways of communication, to carry messages created by the few for everyone in a society with the purpose of informing, influencing, entertaining, and selling.

7. To conclude the lesson, students work in their original small groups to write short descriptions about their medium and to put on mini plays to simulate their mass medium, showing its major functions and characteristics. The rest of the class names the media and functions shown in the mini plays.

8. Pass out copies of Getting to Know Mass Media for students to complete as homework.

Adaptations

- Gifted, upper elementary, and middle school students could conduct research on one medium individually and write a two-page report on functions and characteristics of the medium, then present their report to the class.

- Volunteers from lower elementary, special needs, or ESL classes could identify the correct mass media by labeling them with index cards.

- You may choose to teach from the handouts instead of giving them to children, depending on the age and reading level of your students.

Assessments

- Observe to see whether students can
  —define mass media
  —name two mass media
  —list major functions of mass media

- Assess how well the short passage describes the chosen medium's unique features.

- Evaluate how well the mini plays enable other students to identify the featured medium.

- Evaluate individual completion of Getting to Know Mass Media. (See the answer key on page 151 as a guide to possible answers.)

Getting to Know Mass Media

1. Find two favorite forms of mass media in your house and write what they are below. Briefly explain their features.

    _____
    _____
    _____

2. Give two examples of media programs that give you information.

    _____
    _____
    _____

3. Give two examples from media intended to be primarily entertainment.

    _____
    _____
    _____

4. Give two examples from media that intend to sell you things.

    _____
    _____
    _____

What Goes on Behind the Scenes?

Rationale

Television is one of the most phenomenal of human inventions. It touches lives intimately and pervasively. Before we teach children skills of critical TV viewing, it is important to teach them about television itself, including a brief history of the invention, some basic production techniques, and what goes on behind the scenes of TV programs.

Objectives

- Students will learn about the inventor of television.
- Students will be able to recognize basic production techniques and learn about how programs are made.
- Students will practice TV program making.

Related Content Areas

- ***Language arts:*** Students will understand informational texts, write short TV scripts, read nonfiction, and write a short biography. They will also listen to and speak about TV programming, such as headline news, weather reports, and so forth.

- *Social studies:* Students will learn about the history and inventor of TV.
- *Fine arts:* Students will design, direct, and produce TV programs.

Preparation and Materials

- Bring in a copy of *Philo T. Farnsworth: The Life of Television's Forgotten Inventor*, by Roberts (2003).
- Bookmark or add to the Favorites list on student computers the following Web pages:
  "Philo Farnsworth," by Postman, http://www.time.com/time/time100/scientist/profile/farnsworth.html, and "Biography of Philo T. Farnsworth," by Dekhtyar, http://www.slcc.edu/schools/hum_sci/physics/whatis/biography/farnsworth.html.
  If computers are unavailable, print out these Web articles for students.
- Make copies for students of the TV Production Team (page 27), Basic TV Production Techniques (page 28), and Inventor of Television (page 29) handouts.
- Bring in a copy of the children's book *Television: What's Behind What You See*, by Merbreier (1996).
- Prior to the day you plan to teach the unit, ask students to bring in toy cameras or disposable cameras, if they have them. Or you may provide construction paper and tape to make imaginary cameras for everyone.
- Record examples of television programs: for example, news reports, commercials, weather forecasts, and short dramatic plays from PBS programs such as those in *Barney and Friends*.
- Bring to class a video camera, blank videotapes, and a TV and VCR.
- Arrange a field trip to a local TV studio. If possible, arrange to observe a live news broadcast so that students will see the cameraman, news producer, director, anchor, and reporter in action and learn their roles.
- Estimated time for unit: 6 hours.

Procedure

1. Ask students the following questions and allow a few minutes for discussion:
   - How are TV programs sent to your home?
   - Who makes and sends these programs?

2. To help answer these questions, read aloud to students the book *Television: What's Behind What You See.* Show students the beautiful illustrations that depict what goes on behind the scenes, how programs are made, and how the programs get from TV studio to TV sets.

3. Take a field trip to a local TV studio. Pass out the TV Production Team handout and ask students to identify the roles of the people they see working in the studio. You might want to complete this yourself while at the studio to be sure of which team members students actually see.

4. After the field trip, explain that everything we see on TV or in a movie has been recorded on film or videotapes beforehand. Production teams make decisions about how to produce the show or movie by using various techniques. Explain that students will get hands-on experience of production techniques by using their own cameras outside. If some or all students do not have cameras, have them each roll up a piece of construction paper and tape the edges. Pass out the Basic TV Production Techniques handout.

5. Take the class outside with their cameras and handouts and explain: "We are going to pretend to be camera operators by looking through our cameras." Instruct students to stand still and look straight ahead through their cameras or paper rolls. Ask them the following questions:

   - What do you see?
   - What is in front of you?
   - If you stand still, can you see behind you or to the side of you?

   Come to the understanding that camera operators can see only part of the world but not all through their cameras. They may choose and control what they want to see or show us on TV or in a movie by remaining in certain positions.

6. Go over the Basic TV Production Techniques handout with students and practice these techniques together. Ask students to put the cameras or paper rolls back to their eyes and lead them through the following actions:

   - Have them move their heads slowly to the right. Explain that this horizontal movement across a scene is called a pan.
   - Ask students to stand facing a wall, then to *zoom in* to the wall by moving their heads quickly toward it. Then have them *zoom out* by pulling their heads back quickly.

- Have students look straight ahead at the wall in front and then turn their heads quickly to the left. Explain that this is called a *cut*. A cut is used to end a scene or to end filming.
- Next have students *dissolve* one scene into another by moving their heads away from the wall slowly to the left.
- Finally, have students *fade* by blocking the lenses of the cameras or the ends of the paper rolls with their hands so that they cannot see anything.

7. Back in the classroom, show the prerecorded examples of news reports, commercials, weather forecasts, or short dramatic TV plays.

8. Invite students to make one- or two-minute TV shows in groups, such as a short news report, weather report, short commercial, or familiar story. Each group should have a producer, director, scriptwriter, actors, and cameraperson. Suggest that students decide on topics and kinds of programs first, then write scripts in groups (with the scriptwriter doing the actual writing), while planning how to record each scene before shooting. They should try to use some of the basic techniques they have learned, such as zooming, panning, and cutting.

9. Go over students' drafts of scripts and help them revise before they shoot the programs.

10. Teach or review how to use a video camera before students shoot their mini programs. Students then complete their shows, with groups taking turns to film their programs.

11. Students present their shows to the class. The class reflects on the process of TV program making, including the decision making involved, such as the topic selection process, as well as writing scripts, producing, directing, and shooting. Guide students to the understanding that program makers decide what we see on TV.

12. For the final part of the lesson, ask students whether they have ever wondered who invented TV or how it receives and transmits pictures and sound. Read aloud *Philo T. Farnsworth* to the class.

13. Pass out the Inventor of Television handout and assign the URLs, or pass out printouts, of Postman's and Dekhtyar's Web articles. Have students read the articles and complete the handout as homework.

> **➤ TIP**
>
> *Invite parents to come and watch the students' TV shows as a climax for the study.*

Adaptations

- For lower elementary, special needs, or ESL students, you may want to omit the last step (the Web articles and Inventor of Television handout).
- You may choose to teach from the handouts instead of giving them to children, depending on the age and reading level of your students.
- If a field trip is impossible, invite a TV producer to give a talk.
- For lower elementary, special needs, or ESL students, give more guidance for making short TV shows. You might have the whole class work together and make one TV show.
- If a video camera isn't available, students can perform their shows as skits instead of filming them. Have the cameraperson pretend to do the various techniques (pan, zoom, and so on) as the director calls for them.

Assessments

- Check to see if students complete the TV Production Team handout correctly.
- Observe for participation and successful completion of the mini TV show.
- Check that students complete the Inventor of Television worksheet correctly. (See the answer key on page 151 for guidance.)

TV Production Team

Put a checkmark beside the production team members you see working at the TV studio.

☐ **Program producer:** The producer creates the program and is in charge of writing, music, financial concerns, and hiring the production team. He or she decides who gets to be the camera operator, director, anchor and reporter, or actor.

☐ **Program director:** The director tells the anchor or actor and the camera operator what to do. He or she is the person in charge of everything that takes place while filming and during the editing process.

☐ **Camera operator:** The camera operator films, or "shoots," the programs using the camera.

☐ **Actor or anchor:** The actor or anchor performs or reads the script in front of the camera.

☐ **Scriptwriter:** The scriptwriter writes stories, or scripts—the words that an actor or anchor says in front of the camera.

☐ **Reporter:** A reporter interviews people and writes news stories.

Basic TV Production Techniques

Pan: To move the camera horizontally to see a panorama, an unlimited view.

Zoom in: To quickly move forward to a scene to see it close up.

Zoom out: To quickly move backward (or pull back) from a scene to see it from afar.

Cut: To quickly change from one scene to another, producing a sharp and abrupt feel.

Dissolve: To slowly change from one scene to another, producing a gradual feel by simultaneously fading out of one scene while fading into another.

Fade: To black out or to block the scene completely.

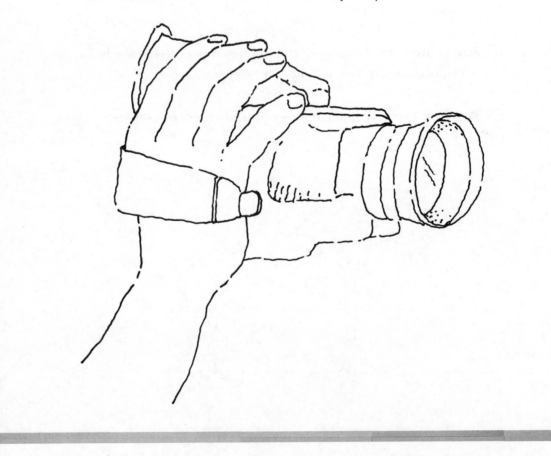

Inventor of Television

1. Read the following:

   - Neil Postman's Web article "Philo Farnsworth" at
     http://www.time.com/time/time100/scientist/profile/farnsworth.html
   - Lyudmila Dekhtyar's Web article "Biography of Philo T. Farnsworth," at
     http://www.slcc.edu/schools/hum_sci/physics/whatis/biography/farnsworth.html

2. Write a story about Philo Farnsworth, the inventor of television, including
   information about his birth date and place, early life, education, inventions and achievements, legal battles, means of recognition, and other
   interesting facts. Continue on the back of this sheet if necessary.

   _____

   _____

   _____

   _____

   _____

   _____

   _____

   _____

   _____

   _____

   _____

   _____

What's the Net?

Rationale

Most children have heard of or experienced the Internet in one way or another; however, it is a good idea to make sure that your students are on the same footing in their understanding of what the Internet is, how information flows on the Internet, and the most commonly used Internet-related terms. This lesson will pave the way for more detailed discussion about the Internet.

Objectives

- Students will be able to define basic terms related to the Internet.
- Students will understand how information flows on the Internet.
- Students will comprehend the open and nonprivate nature of the Internet.

Related Content Areas

- **Language arts:** Students will listen for specific information from literary and informational texts and identify similarities between the two.
- **Science:** Students will learn about the linking nature of spider webs.
- **Fine arts:** Students will express and interpret understanding and meanings through illustrations.

Preparation and Materials

- Make copies for students of the Internet Terms handout (page 33).
- Cut out the 12 terms from the handout to pass out as individual slips.
- Provide art materials (such as crayons, colored pencils, or colored markers and paper) for students to use in drawings.
- Provide little drawings or clip art of computers.
- Bring to class one of the following stories: *Spider Spins a Story: Fourteen Legends from Native America,* by Max (1997); *Charlotte's Web,* by White (2001); or "The Web of Life," by Kid's Planet-Defenders of Wild Life, available at http://www.kidsplanet.org/wol/index.html (Grades 4-6 use *Spider Spins a Story* or *Charlotte's Web.* Grades 2-3 use the "The Web of Life.")
- Gather a few postcards and letters inside envelopes as examples of open and private communications.
- Set up a computer with an Internet connection in a place visible to all students. If possible, connect an overhead projector to the computer so that the computer screen can be enlarged for all students to see clearly.
- Estimated time for unit: 3 hours.

Procedure

1. Explain to students that the topic for discussion will be "the Web." To refresh children's memory of a Web, share a spider story (*Charlotte's Web, Spider Spins a Story,* or "The Web of Life").
2. Discuss the functions of a spider web, pointing out its linking nature and the similarities between a spider web and a computer network.
3. Ask if anyone has seen a real spider web. Ask for a volunteer to draw a big spider web on the board.
4. Pass out the pictures of little computers and ask students to tape them anywhere they want on the spider web.
5. Ask students to think about what the Web and the computers on the board represent. Accept answers such as the Internet, the Net, the World Wide Web, and cyberspace.
6. Explain that the Web represents the Internet, which links many, many computers around the world. Millions of people connect their computers, through telephone lines and cables, to millions of other computers around the world, just like the Web on the board shows. People "talk" to each other through computers in this way. Some people call this shared electronic network the Information Highway or cyberspace.

7. Show the class the postcards and the letters in envelopes. Pass them around. Ask students to suggest all the ways that postcards are different from letters. Be sure that someone notes that postcards are not private; anyone can read them.

8. Ask students, "If you are going to write to someone about a secret, would you choose to use a postcard or a letter?" "Is e-mail more like a letter or a post-card?" Explain the open and nonprivate nature of Internet information and communication.

9. Ask how many students have surfed the Net before and have all students make their own lists of all the things the word "Internet" reminds them of. Choose for discussion the terms that come up frequently in students' lists and introduce the terms from the Internet Terms handout.

10. Have students divide into six small groups and give each group two of the terms you cut out from the handout as well as art supplies. Students read the definitions of the terms and illustrate the terms based on their understanding. Walk around to help with questions.

11. Have the small groups show their illustrations to the class. See if the rest of the class can guess the terms based on the illustrations. Then have the group read the definitions aloud. Be prepared to respond to additional questions students may have about the terms.

12. Give each student a copy of Internet Terms. Go online and show students some examples of the terms on the handout, such as e-mail, chat room, home page, and Web page.

Adaptations

- Introduce only the terms that the children most likely have been exposed to at this age.
- You may choose to teach from the handout instead of giving it to children, depending on the age and reading level of your students.
- An alternative way of introducing the terms of the Internet is to have small groups work on computers. Afterwards, have students show and tell the terms to the class on the computers.

Assessments

- Observe and check understanding from discussion of the spider story and participation in Web making on the board.
- Observe and check understanding from discussion of the open nature of e-mails and online communication.
- Evaluate illustrations of the Internet terms for accuracy.

Internet Terms

Browsers: Software, such as Internet Explorer or Netscape, used to display information on a computer.

Chat room: Electronic "room" where people use computers to talk to each other.

Downloading: Copying a file from another computer to your computer.

E-mail: Stands for "electronic mail." E-mail is a message sent electronically over a computer network.

Internet: Also called "the Net." The network that links many, many computers all over the world.

Modem: Your computer's telephone.

Network: A group of computers that are connected to each other. The Internet is the largest network in the world.

Online: When your computer is connected to the Internet, you are online.

Surfing the Net: Using the Internet to explore Web sites or topics.

Home page: The first thing we see when we open a Web site. It introduces the site to us.

Web page: A single screen in the World Wide Web. A home page is an example of one kind of Web page.

Website: A collection of Web pages that are connected by topic, usually hosted by one person or organization.

World Wide Web: A huge collection of electronic pages containing information about many different subjects. These pages are stored in computers around the world.

What's in a Newspaper?

Rationale

Newspapers are one of the oldest and most popular sources of information in our society. Children see them being read daily at home, in restaurants, at bus stops, on the subway, and many other places. A newspaper provides opportunities for reading, particularly for information and entertainment. It is a good idea to introduce the specific characteristics of newspapers to children early in their lives so that they can fully benefit from them.

Objectives

- Students will recognize different sections of a newspaper and the information in each section.
- Students will recognize local, national, and international news and headlines.
- Students will understand the roles of news and reporters.

Related Content Areas

- *Language arts:* Students will learn how to find main ideas in a news article and be able to define the nature of news and headlines. Students will also conduct research on the Internet.
- *Math:* Students will use division to get average numbers and to calculate total cost.
- *Social studies:* Students will locate various countries and continents and get to know the names of states in the United States.
- *Health:* Students will understand what a healthy diet is and learn about the food pyramid and daily food choices.
- *Fine arts:* Students will express emotions through art projects.

Preparation and Materials

- Collect a variety of local and national newspapers. Gather enough local weekend editions for each pair of students to have one.
- Arrange a field trip to a local newspaper office, particularly the printing area so that students can see the manufacturing process.
- Invite a reporter to speak to the class (at the newsroom or in class).
- Make copies of handouts for all students: What Is in a Newspaper? (page 40), the Food Pyramid (page 41), Grocery Shopping (page 42), Locate the Origins of News (page 43), and Newspapers around the Nation (page 44).
- Set up student computers or a classroom computer, preferably connected to an overhead projector so that all students can see the screen.
- Bookmark or add to the Favorites list the following Web sites on student computers or the classroom computer, or make copies for students of the URLs. Useful kids news sites:

Online Newspapers.com: http://www.onlinenewspapers.com/
Scholastic News: http://teacher.scholastic.com/scholasticnews/
The New York Times on the Web: Learning Network, Grades 3-12:
    http://www.nytimes.com/learning/index.html
Artsonia section of the New York Times on the Web: Learning Network:
    http://www.artsonia.com/affiliates/nytimes/default.asp

- Attach a United States map to a bulletin board.
- Set up a world map or a globe.

- Provide a wide selection of art materials, such as various kinds of paper, scissors, glue, paint, colored pencils, crayons, colored markers, fabric scraps, and anything else you can find to give students a choice in selecting an art project they can complete with the materials on hand.
- Cut up small slips of paper, enough for each student to have two, small enough for the slips to be pinned to a United States map. Have enough thumbtacks or bulletin board pins on hand so that each student will have two.
- Estimated time for unit: 7 hours.

Procedure

1. Introduce the topic of newspapers to the class. Ask students the following questions and write down their answers on the board.

   - What am I holding up? (Hold up a newspaper.)
   - Have you ever read a newspaper before?
   - What newspapers can you name?
   - What is the name of the local newspaper?
   - Who reads newspapers at your home?
   - Why do people read newspapers?
   - What kind of information do you think people get from newspapers?
   - What is news or a news story?
   - What do reporters do?

2. Lead students to an understanding of the following facts:

   - People get local, national, and international news; opinions; information about sales, services, and products; weather reports; sports news; information about what is on TV and playing in local movie theaters; information about cultural events; and other useful information from newspapers.
   - News is factual information about real events reported to people. The news can have many qualities; for example, it can be happy, sad, disturbing, or entertaining.
   - Reporters are people hired by TV networks, news agencies, radio stations, or newspapers to collect news or to find out what is going on locally, nationally, and internationally. Reporters send their stories back to their home offices, or agencies, by telephone, fax, e-mails, and so forth. The agencies will put the news stories received from reporters on air, online, or in newspapers.

3. Introduce the different sections of a newspaper to students by first explaining that newspapers have more than one section. Show students each section of a newspaper and write on the board the names of the major sections (for example, local news, national news, world news, editorial, money, life, sports, classified, weather, and so forth). Show students where to find the index and how to use it as a guide. Show students that important news usually "makes headlines," meaning it appears on the front page and at the top of newspapers. Be sure to clarify that "headlines" also refers to the titles of all news articles in the paper.

4. Have students pair up. Pass out a local weekend edition and the What Is in a Newspaper? handout to each pair of students. Have each pair complete the handout together, then share their answers with the class.

5. The next activity for the unit involves using advertising circulars to teach about healthy food choices and grocery shopping on a budget. Begin by teaching or reviewing food groups using the Food Pyramid handout. Discuss healthy diet and daily food choices with students.

6. Pass out the Grocery Shopping handout and have students work in pairs and pretend that they have $150 to spend for a week's grocery shopping for a family of four. Using the grocery store ads from the weekend issue of a local newspaper, students write shopping lists first and then calculate the cost. Be sure that they include items from each food group: fats, meat, dairy products, fruits, vegetables, and grains.

> **➤ TIP**
>
> *Try hands-on activities, such as puzzles or games, to make learning geography more interesting to students.*

7. Talk about the nutritional factors of the food on their lists and check to see if they follow the food pyramid in grocery shopping.

8. The next activity for the unit helps students understand the connection between news and geography. Review or teach the concept of counties, cities, and states in the United States and continents in the world using a U.S. map and a globe or world map.

9. Pass out the Locate the Origins of News handout and ask students to continue to work with their newspapers to find local, national, and international news and write down on the handout four examples of news stories for each category and the origin of each story. Students can identify either the continents or countries of origin.

10. As a class, locate on a map the origins students wrote down on their hand-outs of local and national news. Then do the same with a world map or globe to locate the origins of the international news students found in their papers.

11. Now that students have a basic understanding of what a newspaper is and how it connects to the world and their lives, the next activity teaches them about how people react to news. Show students examples of student reactions to news through arts at the Artsonia section of the New York Times on the Web: Learning Network. Use a classroom computer with an overhead projector, or have students use computers in pairs (depending on how many computers you have available).

12. Ask students to work in pairs to select a recent important event from the newspaper and react to it through artwork. They may respond to news or world events with an illustration (such as a cartoon) or other project. Encourage students to submit their artwork to Artsonia for publication.

13. Now that students have thoroughly explored a local newspaper, the next activity in the unit introduces them to different newspapers around the country so that they learn that each state has many newspapers. Assign each student two states to work on and pass out the Newspapers around the Nation handout. Have them complete the handout by visiting the Online Newspapers.com Web site. Direct them to the North America, USA section, and have them select "All States." A page listing all states will open up, giving them access to their assigned states. (Students may need to take turns using classroom computers, or you may need to assign this as homework, depending on how many computers your class has access to at one time and the afterschool access of students.)

14. Ask each student to choose one newspaper name for each of the two states he or she explored, print the newspaper names on small slips of paper, and pin the slips on a bulletin board map of the United States, as close to the area each newspaper covers as possible.

15. As closure to the study of newspapers, visit a newspaper office and its printing facility so that students see where and how newspapers are printed. If possible, arrange for a reporter at the office to speak to the students about his or her work experience. Alternatively, arrange for a reporter to come to your classroom.

Adaptations

- For lower elementary, special needs, or ESL students, change the grocery shopping activity so that students pick five things they want to buy and add up the cost.
- You may choose to teach from the handouts instead of giving them to children, depending on the age and reading level of your students. For example, you might omit the Locate the Origins of News handout and activity for younger children.
- For gifted, upper elementary, and middle school students, tie in the inventions of paper making and printing with the newspaper study. Have students visit the Web site Ask Jeeves Kids (http://www.ajkids.com/) for information on these topics.

Assessments

- Check for accurate completion of all handouts.
- Assess student understanding through their successful completion of an art project that reacts to the news.
- Assess understanding through participation in class discussions.

What Is in a Newspaper?

Title of Newspaper: _____

Use the index to examine the newspaper you have and write down the names of the sections. Give an example of a story for each section.

Names of Sections	**Example of Stories**
1. _____	_____
2. _____	_____
3. _____	_____
4. _____	_____
5. _____	_____
6. _____	_____
7. _____	_____
8. _____	_____
9. _____	_____
10. _____	_____
11. _____	_____
12. _____	_____

What news items "made headlines" (are on the front page) in the paper?

1. _____

_____

_____

2. _____

_____

_____

3. _____

_____

_____

The Food Pyramid

The food pyramid is a guide that helps you choose a healthy diet. Use the pyramid to help you eat better every day by choosing a variety of foods to get the nutrients you need and the right amount of each type of food to maintain a healthy weight.

A Daily Healthy Diet

Begin with 6 to 10 servings from the Grains Group: bread, cereal, rice, and pasta.

Add 3 to 5 servings from the Vegetable Group.

Enjoy 2 to 4 servings from the Fruit Group.

Choose 2 to 3 items from the Dairy Group: milk, yogurt, and cheese.

Get protein from 2 to 3 servings of the Meat Group: meat, poultry, fish, dry beans, eggs, and nuts.

Spice your daily diet with very little fats, oils, and sweets.

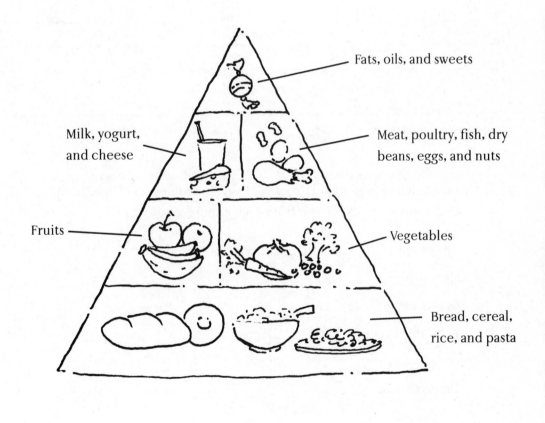

Grocery Shopping

You have $150 to spend for a week's grocery shopping for a family of four. Use your newspaper food ads to write a list of items you want to buy and their prices. Make sure you choose the amounts of foods and types of foods listed in the food pyramid.

Items to Buy	Food Groups	Prices		Items to Buy	Food Groups	Prices
1.				12.		
2.				13.		
3.				14.		
4.				15.		
5.				16.		
6.				17.		
7.				18.		
8.				19.		
9.				20.		
10.				21.		
11.				22.		

Total Cost: $ _____

Saved Amount: $150 – $ _____ = $ _____

How much did you spend for each of the four members of the family?

How many varieties of foods from each group did you buy?

Fat Group: _____

Meat Group: _____

Dairy Group: _____

Vegetable Group: _____

Fruit Group: _____

Grains Group: _____

The Media-Savvy Student © 2004 Zephyr Press, Chicago, IL • (800) 232-2187 • www.zephyrpress.com

Locate the Origins of News

Look through your newspaper and find local, national, and international news. Write the headlines in the chart below. Then try to locate the origins of the news on a map. Write the origin of each story next to its headline in the chart below.

Local News	Origins of News (Counties)
1. _____	_____
2. _____	_____
3. _____	_____
4. _____	_____

National News	Origins of News (States)
5. _____	_____
6. _____	_____
7. _____	_____
8. _____	_____

International News	Origins of News (Continents or Countries)
9. _____	_____
10. _____	_____
11. _____	_____
12. _____	_____

News Around The World

Newspapers Around the Nation

After your teacher assigns you two states to work on, go to the Online Newspapers.com Web site at http://www.onlinenewspapers.com/ and select "All States" from the North America, USA section. Click on the links to your states to find newspapers from each state and answer the questions below.

Names of your states	Total numbers of newspapers for each state	Examples of newspapers	Why did you choose those newspaper examples?

Images in a Digital Age

Rationale

Photography, video, and other film and digital media enable us to use accurate visual records of people, places, and events as a way to interpret the past; however, advances in technology make it easy for anyone to fabricate and manipulate the images available to people. Media are constructed in this way and affect our views of the world. Students need to understand this and learn how to distinguish true images from fabrications.

Objectives

- Students will understand that media are constructed through manipulation of digital images.
- Students will understand that media construct reality through digital images.
- Students will learn firsthand how to create digital images.

Related Content Areas

Fine arts: Students will learn about the art of photography in a digital era and how to visually identify truth from fabrication through an understanding of this art.

Preparation and Materials

- Install image-manipulation software on your computer and practice using it so that you are able to make changes to a digital image before teaching this to students.

- Bookmark or add to your Favorites list the online article "Photographic Truth in the Digital Era," available on the Media Awareness Network Web site at http://www.media-awareness.ca/english/resources/educational/teachable_ moments/photo_truth.cfm. For a detailed analysis of the World Trade Center photo discussed in this article, see the Urban Legends Web site at http://www.urbanlegends.com/ulz/lastmoment.html.

- Review the online article "Ethics in the Age of Digital Photography," by the National Press Photographers Association (2000), at http://www.nppa.org/ services/ bizpract/eadp/eadp8.html.

- Gather copies of digitally manipulated pictures and some digital pictures to be manipulated by students. Both online articles mentioned above have examples of digitally manipulated pictures. Students may have digital pictures they can bring in on disk, or they can use print photographs and a scanner (if you have one available). You could also download pictures from the Internet before class, but be sure to read the fine print (often called Terms of Use) to make sure you are not violating copyright by downloading and manipulating the images in class.

> **➤ TIP**
>
> *Digital cameras usually come with photo manipulation software that you can use.*

- Make a copy of the Change the Look of a Photo (page 49) handout for each student.

- Before you begin the unit, ask students to bring in favorite photos to share.

- Estimated time for unit: 2 to 3 hours.

Procedure

1. Invite students to share their favorite photos. Then show them some digitally manipulated pictures, such as those from the Web sites mentioned in Preparation and Materials or your own creations: for example, a dog with a human body, or your own picture with a mustache or a clown hat. Ask students if they think these are real photos. If you use pictures of yourself, ask if they can recognize you, and if they can tell what makes you look like that.

2. Check to see if any students have used a digital camera or any photo or art software such as Adobe Photoshop or Adobe Photo Deluxe. On your computer, open up image-manipulation software and show students how you cut and paste to change the look of an image.

3. Explain to students that digital technology allows anyone with a computer and image-manipulation software to cut and paste a wide range of images and alter the look of photos. People can manipulate images by using special effects to distort, switch bodies, combine two photos, or disguise a person in a photo by adding glasses, mustaches, hats, or other props.

4. Discuss as a class:

   - Can we believe everything we see in media images?
   - Why is it especially important to learn to tell truth from fabrication in photos that appear to be real?
   - How about videos, DVDs, and movies in the theater? Can they be fabricated in the same way?

> **➤ TIP**
>
> *The Media Awareness Network article "Photographic Truth in the Digital Era" shows an excellent example of the ease and seriousness of digital manipulation: the manipulated picture of a tourist standing on the World Trade Center a minute before the tragedy of September 11 happened. Supposedly, the camera containing the shot was found in the rubble of the Twin Towers. It didn't take long to discover that this image was from a digitally manipulated Web photo gallery. You may discover how the picture was manipulated as a class by using collage to add an airplane, a man, a date, and a time to a picture of buildings.*

Come to the understanding that we need to learn to tell truth from fabrication in this digital age; that media are constructed through digital technology; and that they in turn construct reality to affect our views of the world. Help students understand that videos, DVDs, and movies can be manipulated in the same way.

5. Give students some time to work with image-manipulation software to alter the look of one photo for hands-on experience. They could use digital pictures or scan in photos of themselves.
   Ideas for the activity:

   - Add objects (such as a car, cell phone, ballet shoes, or makeup) to the image of a historical person.
   - Use a photo of a child roller skating and paste in a piece of cloud so that it looks as if he or she is skating high in the sky.
   - Switch bodies between a photo of an animal and a photo of a human.
   - Make a city out of one building by copying and pasting that building repeatedly.

6. Students share their manipulated photos with the class and explain the techniques they used.

Adaptations

- Lower elementary, special needs, or ESL students may manipulate photos by literally cutting and pasting.
- For gifted, upper elementary, and middle school students, tie in knowledge of the history and invention of photography.
- You may choose to teach from the handout instead of giving it to children, depending on the age and reading level of your students.

Assessments

- Observe in discussion whether students understand that media are constructed and construct reality.
- Check to see if students are able to use software to change the look of photos.
- Check student work on the Change the Look of a Photo handout.

Change the Look of a Photo

1. What software are you using?

   _____

   _____

2. What photo or image are you working on?

   _____

   _____

3. What techniques are you using? (For example, distortion, body switching, combining two photos, trick scale, disguises, duplicating, and so on.)

   _____

   _____

   _____

4. How does the photo look now?

   _____

   _____

5. What is the effect of the change?

   _____

   _____

Media Culture Through the Eyes of Alien Friends

Rationale

In our media-prevalent society, it is a good idea to stand back and look at media from another perspective, an alien perspective, which will further help our students understand the media culture of our society.

Objectives

- Students will better understand the nature of a media society.
- Students will understand individual medium's characteristics from a new perspective.
- Students will write science fiction or factual reports.

Related Content Areas

- **Language arts:** Students will understand the differences between factual and fictional writings; write factual and fictional descriptions; learn conventions and mechanics of writing; and learn the process of writing:

drafting, editing, revising, and publishing. Students will also listen and speak during presentations.

- **Science:** Students will understand basic human anatomy and the five senses.
- **Fine arts:** Students will design and make models of media using various materials.

Preparation and Materials

- Gather the following books: the science fiction story *The Magic School Bus Inside the Human Body*, by Cole and Degen (1990), and the informational book *My Five Senses*, by Brandenberg (1990).
- Gather art materials for students to use in making models of real and imaginary mass media. For example, boxes of various sizes, empty containers (such as margarine tubs and coffee cans), construction paper, glue, scissors, fabric scraps, pipe cleaners, modeling clay, straws, and anything you can find that might spark student imagination.
- Estimated time for unit: 5 hours.

Procedure

1. Talk about the difference between science fiction and realistic fiction, and the difference between imaginative and informational writings. Read aloud *The Magic School Bus Inside the Human Body* and *My Five Senses* to the class.

2. Compare the books so that students see the differences between imaginative (science fiction/fantasy) and informational writings. The imagined Magic School Bus carrying Ms. Frizzle and the entire class shrinks and is accidentally eaten by Arnold. Through an imaginary journey in Arnold, the Magic School Bus shows us the inside of a human body. We call this type of book science fiction or fantasy. *My Five Senses* is a factual, accurate, and informational recount of the five senses of human beings.

3. As a class, briefly summarize and outline the main ideas and information of both books—basic anatomy of the human body and the five senses.

4. Tell the class that you will work on informational (factual) and imaginary (fictional) investigations of media. Divide the class into two big groups: Earth Friends and Alien Friends. Each big group should then form three or four small groups. Earth Friends will conduct real research and write factual or informational reports, while Alien Friends will use their imagination to write reports about imaginary media used on their planets.

5. Earth Friends groups each pick one popular mass medium to study. Students conduct research on and write brief descriptions of their chosen media, including history, appearance, function, and how people use them. They make models to go with the reports. Throughout the project, they should keep in mind that they need to make sure the Alien Friends can understand the reports and the models.

6. Alien Friends groups imagine and write about mass media forms that residents on other planets use—what the media look like, how people use them, their functions, and their impact on residents of these planets. These groups also make models of the media to go with their explanations.

7. Students work in groups on writing the drafts, revising, and editing their writings in writing workshops.

8. Students from both big groups show and tell about their mass media models and hand in their writings.

> **➤ TIP**
>
> *Alien Friends may choose to dress up in alien clothes and masks.*

Adaptations

- For lower elementary, special needs, or ESL students, this lesson can be adapted to descriptions of one mass medium with pictures instead of models.

- Upper elementary, middle school, and gifted students could write a story about aliens and earthlings meeting, incorporating mass media from earth and other planets in the story.

- Upper elementary, middle school, and gifted students could describe to other groups their various media without naming them and see if the other groups can build each medium based on the description.

Assessments

- Check that writings describe the characteristics of media well, with all required information, and are free of mechanical errors. The Earth Friends writings should meet the requirements of factual writings, and the Alien Friends should meet the requirements of fictional writings.

- Evaluate models for creativity and clear representation of media characteristics.

- Check that presentations are clear and thought provoking.

2

Becoming Critical Viewers

Today's children grow up with television, videos and DVDs, and movies in these formats as well as in the theater. Viewing plays an important role in their lives. These media are a source of entertainment, information, models of behavior, values, attitudes, and lifestyle patterns; and they often function as baby-sitters. Television's live broadcast encourages children to think what they see is true, rather than a construction of reality. Often children do not think deeply about or question what they see on television or in movies. They use the time they could spend forming friendships, playing games, and talking with family members on television instead.

We want children to understand and to be skeptical about what they view. By understanding the political, social, and economic influences of what they see, children will have the power to change the way they respond to and interact with media. This chapter provides ideas for showing children how to analyze programs critically and become more sophisticated critics. The units teach children how to distinguish fantasy from reality, identify stereotypes, and talk back to TV. They help children understand how TV constructs reality, the political impact of media, and why people interpret the same program differently.

We Are Smarter than TV

Rationale

Many of us depend on TV for entertainment, news, education, and culture; however, there are programs of good quality and those of inappropriate and poor quality. Children need to learn how to seek out high quality TV programs and enjoy them. Learning active and critical-viewing skills helps children understand that they are smarter than television. They can make up their own minds about the power and influence of television. Armed with critical-viewing skills, children are encouraged to take action regarding programs they watch instead of being passive viewers.

Objectives

- Students will learn the three steps of critical viewing.
- Students will identify thoughts and feelings about programs and take action based on these thoughts and feelings.
- Students will demonstrate skeptical attitudes and reactions to TV programs.

Related Content Areas

- **Language arts:** Students will describe verbally their feelings about and reactions to television and will make a class book. Students will also participate in class sharing and responding.
- **Fine arts:** Students will learn and practice cartoon illustration.

Preparation and Materials

- Make copies for students of the How Do You Feel About the Programs? handout (page 59).
- Provide enough drawing materials for students to use in creating cartoons (such as pencils, pens, colored markers, and paper).
- Create or buy a binder to use in creating a class book of student illustrations.
- Estimated time for unit: 3 hours.

Procedure

1. Introduce the topic by asking students:

   - Is everything on TV true?
   - Is everything on TV good for you?
   - Can you name some feelings that TV sparks in you?

2. Ask students, "When someone on TV has said something really silly or unbelievable, have you ever felt like talking back to him or her?" Ask students what they would say to this commercial:

   The vitamin D–enriched crunchy chocolate bar with creamy caramel makes a perfect healthy snack for you!

   Write down students' answers: They might say such things as "I don't believe it." "It can't be true." "What? A chocolate bar is a healthy snack?"

3. Introduce the model for critical viewing. It has three steps:

   - Decide your feelings and thoughts about the show. How do you feel about it? How does it make you feel?
   - Tell your TV directly how you feel about it and how it makes you feel.
   - Take action, such as to keep watching, talk back, turn it off, or write to or call the program directors.

4. Brainstorm with the class how one may feel and think about TV programs and list these feelings and thoughts on the board. See the How Do You Feel About the Programs? handout for examples.

5. Brainstorm with the class ways that people can talk back to TV programs; practice talking back as a class. Here are some examples of ways to talk back to the TV based on various thoughts and feelings:

    -   It's too hard for me. I cannot understand it.
    -   It's not fair. I won't watch it anymore.
    -   This is too scary for me. I will turn it off.
    -   It's boring. I will go outside to play.
    -   It's not true. I will call or write to the director of the program about it.
    -   This program shows me how to make friends. I will watch it again.
    -   It makes me laugh. He is just like my dad.
    -   We learned about that bird at school, but I have never seen it. I will keep watching.

6. Next have students recall or make up TV programs that have or would make them feel negative. Have them describe and illustrate their program examples in cartoon style and share their illustrations and descriptions with the class. You may wish to teach or review cartoon drawing.

7. During the sharing, invite the class to practice talking back to their illustrated TV programs and to the program makers. Have students take notes about what others say about the programs they illustrated and write these comments on their illustrations. This kind of sharing will empower students with ways to react to the negative feelings their examples evoke.

8. Put the student illustrations and descriptions (with talk-back comments) together in a class book titled *Talking Back to TV Programs*. Keep it in the class library for everyone to see.

9. Tell students that now they have become TV critics. Pass out the handout How Do You Feel About the Programs? and ask students to examine the TV programs they watch for a week and record their reactions. Discuss with the class what they will do when they feel negative about a program they watch. Encourage students to watch programs they feel positive about and to talk back to or turn off the TV when they start to feel negative about any programs. They can do it because they are smarter than TV! When the homework is handed in, ask students to share their experiences and responses in small groups.

Adaptations

- Challenge gifted, upper elementary, and middle school students by asking them to take the action of writing to a local TV station or program director to explain their feelings about a certain program.
- Depending on the age and reading level of your students, you may choose to assign the handout topic without passing out the handout itself, or adapt the handout to your students' vocabulary.

Assessments

- Evaluate each student's contribution of a page to the class book with one cartoon illustration, description of a TV program, and a list of ways to talk back to it.
- Check students' understanding of the three-step model of critical viewing through their participation in discussion.
- Check students' understanding of the critical-viewing model through their completion of the homework How Do You Feel About the Programs?

How Do You Feel About the Programs?

While you watch TV this week, write down the titles of the programs, your thoughts and feelings about them, and your reactions to them (what you say or do in response to your thoughts and feelings). Use the following list as a guide.

Positive Thoughts and Feelings	*Negative Thoughts and Feelings*
Funny	Not funny
Exciting	Boring
Educational	Not inspiring
Adventurous	Unpleasant
Entertaining	Too many put-downs
True	Not true
Smart	Unfair (e.g., nicer to boys than to girls)
Imaginative	Unimaginative
Creative	Annoying; too many commercials
Interesting	Too much fighting and killing
Understandable; made for kids	Hard to understand; made for adults
Makes me feel good about myself	Makes me feel bad about myself
Can identify with and relate to	Cannot identify with or relate to
Don't want to miss it next time	Waste of time

	Dates	Titles	Thoughts and Feelings	Reactions
1.				
2.				
3.				
4.				
5.				
6.				
7.				
8.				
9.				
10.				

Countering Violence in Media

Rationale

Media violence is one factor that contributes to aggression and violence in our society. Because violence sells, there is more violence in the reel world than in the real world. Media portrayals that tend to legitimize, normalize, trivialize, or glorify violence suggest to children that this behavior has few negative consequences. Media violence affects children by increasing their aggressive behaviors and their appetite for more violence in entertainment and in real life. Careful examination and understanding of violence in media is an important factor in the prevention of violent and other at-risk behaviors.

Objectives

- Students will recognize violence in media.
- Students will recognize differences between real and fictional violence.
- Students will become aware of alternatives to violence.

Related Content Areas

- **Language arts:** Students will write, edit, revise, and publish an expository paper; make a difference by writing to a local newspaper; and use children's literature to learn problem solving.
- **Math:** Students will use division to calculate average instances of violence in a given time.
- **Fine arts:** Students will illustrate an expository paper.

Preparation and Materials

- Set up a TV, VCR, or DVD player, and an overhead projector in your classroom.
- Bring in a video or DVD of the cartoon *Tom and Jerry Kids—S.O.S. in Ninja* (1992), by St. John. Note the length of the cartoon in minutes.
- Bring in a video or DVD of the movie *Hero* (2003), by Zhang. You will need to watch the movie first to find the parts described in steps 7 and 8 below. If

using a video, set the tape to start at the scene described in step 7 and make note of where on the VCR counter the scene described in step 8 begins so that you can find that scene quickly in class. If using a DVD, simply note which scene numbers to select.

- Create an overhead transparency of Violence in Media (page 64).
- Make copies for students of the Violence Track Sheet (page 65) handout.
- Review the National Institute on Media and the Family online fact sheet "Children and Media Violence," available at http://www.mediafamily.org/facts/facts_vlent.shtml.
- Gather the following children's books: *Hands Are Not for Hitting*, by Agassi (2000); *When Sophie Gets Angry, Really, Really Angry*, by Bang (2000); and *We Can Work It Out: Conflict Resolution for Children*, by Polland (2001).
- Teach the genre of expository writing before beginning this unit (or see the alternatives in the Adaptations section on page 63).
- Provide drawing materials for students to use in illustrating their writing (such as crayons, markers, colored pencils, and paper).
- Estimated time for unit: 5 hours.

Procedure

1. Discuss with students what violence is and how many types of violence there are. Ask students the following questions:

   - What examples of violence can you think of?
   - What kinds of violence have you ever seen or heard before?
   - In what media do you see violence often?
   - Do you see more violence in real life or on TV?
   - How do you feel about violence?

2. Put the Violence in Media transparency on the overhead and discuss further what violence is and any examples that students didn't volunteer.

3. Pass out the Violence Track Sheet handout and show *Tom and Jerry Kids—S.O.S. in Ninja*. Ask students to record instances of violence on the Violence Track Sheet while watching the cartoon.

4. Teach or review the concept of using division to figure out averages. Tell students how long the cartoon was and have them calculate the average instances of violence per minute (or per hour).

5. Discuss with students:

> ➤ **TIP**
>
> *Use any available and familiar cartoon, news report, sports program, or drama program that contains violence instead of the suggested ones. Consider expanding this unit to cover video games as well.*

- Why do Tom and Jerry always come out unharmed no matter what they do to each other?
- What would happen to you if you were hit on the head by a spade or fell from a flagpole?
- What are the differences between violence on TV and real violence?
- What will happen in real life if someone commits a serious violent act?
- How does violence help in solving problems?
- What alternatives to violence can you suggest to solve problems?

Come to the understanding that it is impossible in real life for someone to experience the kind of violence that Tom and Jerry do (being hit on the head, falling from high buildings, bumping into doors) and come out unharmed. The cartoon does not show the real consequences of violence. It exaggerates, trivializes, glamorizes, and legitimizes violence to entertain children. In reality, there are serious consequences for committing violent acts. People involved in violence may get hurt by, feel sad about, or die from it. People who act violently may go to jail or be executed for the act. Violence is not a good way to solve problems; there are alternatives, such as understanding, compromising, talking, and forgiving.

6. Show the transparency Violence in Media on the overhead again. Explain the role of violence in media.
7. As an example for alternatives to violence, show the part of the movie *Hero* when the assassin, Nameless, changes his mind and lets the king live as an alternative to killing him. As a result, the king was able to unify China more than 2000 years ago. Invite students to talk about instances when they decided to solve problems with nonviolent measures.
8. As an example of glamorized and trivialized violence, show the part of *Hero* when Gaoshan (meaning mountain) tries to prove his love for Liushui (meaning waterfall) in a disagreement by running into her sword. Liushui then joins him by killing herself with the same sword. After showing this, discuss with students:

- How did Gaoshan and Liushui handle their conflict?
- Was it appropriate?
- Can you suggest an alternative? Are there better ways to handle conflict in real life?

Point out to students that the movie glamorizes the suicidal act of the two and trivializes the consequences. Lead students to the understanding that it was very foolish for the couple to disrespect and waste their own lives for nothing. In real life, sensible people do not prove their love for each other by giving up their lives. As a class, discuss alternatives for the couple to solve their problem appropriately instead of using violence.

9. Read aloud to students the two children's books *Hands Are Not for Hitting* and *When Sophie Gets Angry, Really, Really Angry*. Conduct an open discussion on how students think of the two stories and how they relate to the stories.

10. Invite students to write an expository paper explaining their opinions about violence, consequences of violence, alternatives to violence in solving problems, and how they would persuade people to resort to peaceful measures. Have students use Polland's *We Can Work It Out: Conflict Resolution for Children* (2001) as a reference for ideas. Students work in pairs to edit each other's draft, then each student illustrates his or her writing as well.

11. Have the class publish their expository papers with illustrations by sharing them and reading aloud to each other or by sending their papers to a local newspaper.

Adaptations

- Instead of writing the expository paper, lower elementary, special needs, or ESL students may make a list of the consequences of violence and alternatives.

- Instead of calculating the instances of violence per minute, lower elementary, special needs, or ESL students may simply add up the instances of violence in the program.

- You may choose to teach from the transparency instead of displaying it to children, depending on the age and reading level of your students.

Assessments

- Check accurate completion of the Violence Track Sheet (including the brief descriptions). See the answer key on page 152 for guidance (if you use the suggested Tom and Jerry cartoon).

- Check understanding through participation in and contribution to discussion.

- Check for correct calculation of the instances of violence in the program shown.

- Evaluate expository writing for understanding, fulfillment of requirements, and mechanical correctness.

Violence in Media

What is violence?

Any actions or words intended to hurt someone emotionally or physically; for example, when a person hits someone or says something that makes a person feel sad or scared.

Types of violence

Examples of physical violence: pushing, shoving, hitting, punching, kicking, biting, throwing things at, shooting, stabbing, vandalism, and so on

Examples of emotional violence: name-calling, yelling, threatening, put-downs, and dumping (taking out anger on another person who didn't cause the anger)

What is the role of violence in media?

Media producers use sensational, odd, weird, bizarre, and violent people and situations to keep audiences interested so that they continue to watch. Media exaggerate for dramatic effect. As a result they make violence seem trivial, normal, glamorous, and legitimate. Media often depict violence that is out of the ordinary. We should understand

- there is more violence in the reel world than in the real world;
- violence is not the norm nor typical of our lives;
- violence has consequences and violent people are punished;
- violence is not an acceptable way to settle conflict in real life; peaceful solutions to conflict are always preferable to retaliation (getting back at someone) and violence.

Violence Track Sheet

Watch the program your teacher shows to your class, and every time you see violence, describe it in the spaces below. Write each new instance of violence next to a new number.

Description of Violence

1. _____
   _____

2. _____
   _____

3. _____
   _____

4. _____
   _____

5. _____
   _____

6. _____
   _____

7. _____
   _____

8. _____
   _____

9. _____
   _____

10. _____
   _____

11. _____
   _____

Length of the program: _____

Number of violent instances: _____

Average violence per minute: _____

Can They Really Do That?

Rationale

Media create reality in which they make the impossible possible and mix fantasy with reality to glamorize reality and entertain the audience. Children will be less affected by or be immune to such portrayal if they know it is fictional. To distinguish fantasy from reality is a useful skill for children to learn.

Objectives

- Students will distinguish fantasy from reality.
- Students will understand how a superhero is made in a studio, and this understanding will help them to become critical of media fiction.

Related Content Areas

- **Language arts:** Students will read for comprehension and understanding and compare fantasy with reality.
- **Social studies:** Students will learn world history through study of a Chinese historical figure, Emperor Qin, and his time.
- **Physical education:** Students will understand what gong fu is and how it is different from wrestling, karate, judo, and tae kwon do.

Preparation and Materials

- Make or buy a superhero costume for yourself.
- Set up a TV and VCR or DVD player in the classroom.

- Bring in the movie *Hero* (2003), by Zhang. (You will need two hours' class time for viewing and discussion.)
- Bring in the children's book *Bionic Bunny Show,* by Brown (1984).
- Make copies for students of Programs with Reality and Fantasy (page 69), Fantasy in *Hero* (page 70), and *Hero* Discussion Guide (page 71) handouts.
- Before starting the unit, read the online article "People: Qin Shihuang–the First Emperor in Chinese History," available at http://www.chinavoc.com/history/qin/qinshh.htm
- Bring in a TV guide or the TV listings section of a newspaper (optional).
- If possible, provide computers with online access and PowerPoint software installed for all students or for the class to share. If not possible, provide materials for students to create visual displays (such as poster board and markers).
- Estimated time for unit: 6 to 7 hours.

Procedure

1. Introduce the topic by coming to the classroom dressed as a superhero. Ask students if they believe that you fly in through an open window. Why or why not? Explain the difference between fantasy and realistic fiction.

    - Fantasy fiction depicts scenes and events that cannot happen in the real world. They only occur in an imaginary, or fictional, world. Fantasy makes the unbelievable look believable. Examples include the Harry Potter series, by J.K. Rowling, and the Red Wall series, by Brian Jacques.
    - Realistic fiction depicts scenes and events that could (and often do) happen in everyday life in the real world. Examples include *Superfudge* (1980) and *Tales of a Fourth Grade Nothing* (1972), by Judy Blume; *Herbie Jones Superhero* (1989), by Suzy Kline; and *Bridge to Terabithia,* by Katherine Paterson.

2. Pass out the Programs with Reality and Fantasy handout. Have students work in pairs to think of some examples for each category. They may use a TV guide as a reference for general types of programs and specific program titles.

3. Ask if any students have taken karate or gong fu (also known as kung fu or gung fu) lessons before. Ask them to share their experiences if they have. Tell students that they will watch a movie with gong fu in it. Explain what gong fu is briefly. For guidance, see numbers 5 and 6 in the answer key for the *Hero* Discussion Guide, on page 153.

4. Pass out the handout Fantasy in *Hero*. Show the movie *Hero* and have students take notes on the handout of events, scenes, acts, or characters that they believe to be unreal and fantastic.

5. After the movie, have students share notes in small groups.

6. Pass out the *Hero* Discussion Guide and discuss the questions with students. (See the answer key on page 153 for guidance in helping students answer the questions.)

7. Read aloud the story *Bionic Bunny Show*. It helps students to distinguish between fantasy and reality and gives them a look at how a superhero TV show is made. Discuss how Wilbur, an ordinary rabbit, is transformed into the Bionic Bunny by means of make-up, special effects, and camera techniques.

8. To conclude the unit, have students choose from the following topics and conduct research in the library or online, using multiple resources.

   - Qin Shihuang and Qin Dynasty
   - Terra cotta soldiers
   - Xian, the ancient capital of Qin
   - Gong fu

   If students have access to PowerPoint, have them present their studies to the class using that software. If they don't have access, have students prepare an oral presentation using visual aids.

> **➤ TIP**
>
> *For extra credit, have students design their own fake superhero by presenting (in writing or performance) the superhero's powers and how they are created using special effects.*

Adaptations

- For lower elementary, special needs, or ESL students, the research project may be adapted to finding one book or one resource from the library or the Internet about the topic and talking about it with the class.
- You may choose to teach from the handouts instead of giving them to children, depending on the age and reading level of your students.

Assessments

- Check if students give correct examples for each category of TV programs on the Programs with Reality and Fantasy handout. (See the answer key on page 152 for answer examples.)
- Check that students are able to correctly identify fantasy events, actions, and characters from *Hero* on the Fantasy in *Hero* handout.
- Evaluate student research and presentations on the suggested topics for ample information and effective presentation.

Programs with Reality and Fantasy

Give at least two examples for each category listed below. In your pairs, discuss the characteristics that distinguish reality-based from fantasy-based TV shows and movies.

Programs with real events:

_____

_____

_____

Programs with actors and actresses:

_____

_____

_____

Programs with real people:

_____

_____

_____

Programs with animation:

_____

_____

_____

Programs with combinations (real person/actor and animation):

_____

_____

_____

Programs that are reality-based:

_____

_____

_____

Programs that are fantasy-based:

_____

_____

_____

Fantasy in Hero

Watch the movie and take notes below of the events, characters, and actions that you think are unreal and fantastic.

1. _____
   _____
   _____

2. _____
   _____
   _____

3. _____
   _____
   _____

4. _____
   _____
   _____

5. _____
   _____
   _____

6. _____
   _____
   _____

7. _____
   _____
   _____

8. _____
   _____
   _____

9. _____
   _____
   _____

10. _____
    _____
    _____

Hero *Discussion Guide*

1. Who was Emperor Qin?

2. What time period did he live in?

3. Why was he important in Chinese history?

4. Where is his tomb?

5. What is gong fu?

6. How is gong fu different from wrestling, karate, judo, or tae kwon do?

7. Do you believe that the superheroes in the movie really fight with each other while flying over mountains and walking on water and on top of trees?

8. Can the heroes really block iron arrows with their bodies?

9. How does a movie production team make them do that?

10. Is it possible or believable that Emperor Qin would give a sword to the assassin and let him choose whether or not to kill the emperor?

11. Did Gaoshan and Liushui in real life die from the sword?

12. Do you wish to see a different ending to the movie? How do you want the story to end differently?

We Make the World

Rationale

People do not soak in everything they see, read, or hear. They get involved in programs with different levels of understanding because of who they are and what life experiences they bring to viewing. People with diverse backgrounds may come up with different perceptions, perspectives, and feelings about the same program. To be sensitive to how media affects different people, students need to understand that audiences participate in making meaning.

Objectives

- Students will understand the role of audience in meaning making.
- Students will learn that individual experiences affect meaning making.
- Students will understand that audiences do not receive but conceive meaning.
- Students will demonstrate the ability to see other perspectives when identifying different readers' responses to familiar story lines.

Related Content Areas

- *Language arts:* Students will read and comprehend multicultural children's legends and folktales; compare variations of folktales; research using various resources; and organize information into a report. Students will also participate in discussion and presentation.
- *Social studies:* Students will learn about Chinese culture and Chinese history.

Preparation and Materials

- Provide copies of the children's book *Cinderella* (1989), by John Patience, for each student or pair of students.
- Make copies for students of the *Mulan* Viewing Guide (page 76) and *Mulan* Venn Diagram (page 77) handouts.
- Set up a TV and VCR or DVD player in your classroom.
- Bring in a video or DVD of Disney's *Mulan* (1998).
- Bring in a copy of "The Ballad of Mulan," by Zhang (1998).
- Provide student copies of *Disney's Mulan: Classic Storybook*, by Marsoli (1998), for younger students, or *Disney's Mulan: Junior Novel*, by Dubowski (1998), for older students.
- Before the unit, learn more about Mulan at Kuo's "The Mulan FAQ" (2002) at http://www.geocities.com/Hollywood/5082/mulanfaq.html.
- If possible, provide computers with PowerPoint installed for student use.
- Estimated time for unit: 6 to 7 hours.

Procedure

1. Ask student volunteers to tell the class what programs they remember watching recently. Did they like them? Why or why not? Join the discussion by sharing one or two of your favorite programs.
2. Ask students to recall the story of Cinderella. Briefly review the story together.
3. Ask students:

   - Did you like the story when you were younger?
   - What do you think of the story now?
   - How would you feel about the story if you were a stepsister, stepbrother, stepmother, or stepfather?

4. Discuss ways in which different readers might respond to the story; for example, young children, older boys, older girls, psychologists, stepmothers, stepsisters, and feminists.

5. Pass out copies of Patience's *Cinderella* and have students read the story. Divide them into four groups and ask them to respond to the story pretending to be young children, psychologists, stepmothers, feminists, or other readers who may have an interesting response to the story. Students may choose to respond to the text orally or in writing.

   As students respond to the story, encourage them to consider the personal values, perspectives, and experiences of the person they pretend to be. For instance, a psychologist might focus on issues regarding Cinderella's upbringing, such as the effects that childhood mistreatment might have on her as an adult. A feminist might focus on the female stereotypes, such as the dependent princess, vain stepsisters, and evil stepmothers. A young child might identify with feeling insecure living among a stepfamily. When all students have responded, conclude by discussing how different personal values, perspectives, and experiences may influence different readers' responses to the same text.

6. Pass out the *Mulan* Viewing Guide handout and ask students to answer the questions in part I, then share their answers in small groups.

7. Play the video or DVD of *Mulan*. Afterwards, ask students to answer the questions in part II, then share their answers with the class.

8. Read aloud "The Ballad of Mulan" to the class. After the story, pass around copies of *Disney's Mulan: Classic Storybook* or *Disney's Mulan: Junior Novel* to small groups and ask students to use the *Mulan* Venn Diagram handout to compare Disney's version of Mulan with the original Mulan story. (Students should write similarities in the center of the diagram and differences in the outer parts of the diagram.)

9. After students complete the *Mulan* Venn Diagram, ask students the questions on the *Mulan* Discussion Guide, on page 78, and discuss their answers. Use the discussion guide sample answers to guide the discussion as necessary.

10. Have students answer the questions in part III of the *Mulan* Viewing Guide and share their answers in small groups.

11. To conclude the lesson, students work in small groups on a research report. Each group picks one topic to research. For example:

- Mulan and her time
- Dragons in Chinese culture

As a group, students take notes on information and use those notes to write a two-page report. If possible, have each group make a PowerPoint presentation to the class.

Adaptations

- For lower elementary, special needs, or ESL students, you may want to give more guidance in the final project, or you may choose to share another Chinese legend or dragon story instead.
- You may choose to teach from the handouts instead of giving them to children, depending on the age and reading level of your students.

> **TIP**
>
> *Alternatively, students could work on finding and presenting three ancient Chinese poems or one Chinese folktale or legend.*

Assessments

- Check student understanding through their answers on the *Mulan* Viewing Guide.
- Check to see if the *Mulan* Venn Diagram is completed with comprehension. (See the sample answers in the answer key on page 77.)
- Check student understanding through participation in class discussions.
- Evaluate successful completion of the research project.

Mulan *Viewing Guide*

I. *Before watching the video:*

1. What do you know about Mulan, the movie and the person?

   _____

   _____

2. What are your expectations for the movie?

   _____

   _____

II. *After watching the video:*

3. How do you feel about the movie? What are your opinions, thoughts, and conclusions about the movie? _____

   _____

4. Can you explain why you think and feel about the movie the way you do? What in your life leads you to these thoughts and feelings?

   _____

   _____

III. *After class discussion:*

5. What did you learn from the discussion about the movie and Mulan that you did not know before? _____

   _____

6. Now that you have watched the movie, read the original story of Mulan. Do you think and feel the same way about the movie as you did before?

   _____

   _____

7. Have you arrived at any new thoughts, opinions, and feelings about the Disney movie? If yes, what are they? _____

   _____

8. What in this class led you to these new thoughts and feelings?

   _____

   _____

9. How do you think your new knowledge and experience help you understand the movie? _____

   _____

Mulan *Venn Diagram*

Read the two versions of the Mulan story and compare them. Write the similarities and differences in the following Venn diagram.

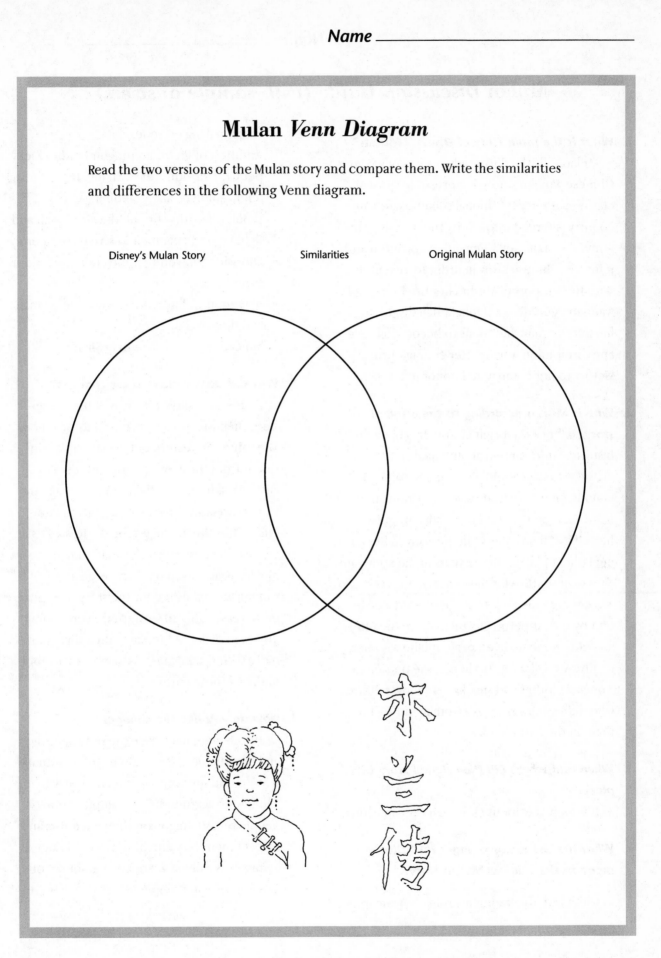

Disney's Mulan Story   Similarities   Original Mulan Story

Mulan *Discussion Guide (with sample answers)*

1. What is the main story of Disney's Mulan?

Mulan tells the daring adventures of a young Chinese woman whose irrepressible spirit clashes with her traditional society. When her country is forced into war by the invading Hun army, she takes her ailing father's position and joins the Chinese army in order to save his life. With the support of Mushu, her fire-breathing, wannabe guardian dragon, Mulan disguises herself as a man and trains to become a brave and disciplined warrior. Her courage brings victory to her country and honor to her family.

2. Who is Mulan according to the original story? (Check the original story by Zhang for historical information about Mulan.)

Mulan, a 17-year-old girl, is the heroine of a famous Chinese narrative verse written about 1,500 years ago. In the story, Mulan disguises herself as a man to serve in the army in her ailing father's place. After 12 years in the army, she wins many battles for the country, is recognized as a courageous soldier, and is offered a position by the emperor. She turns down the offer and goes home to live a peaceful life with her family. After she returns home, she puts on her woman's clothes and shocks her fellow soldiers, who didn't know she was a woman during the time on the battlefield.

3. When and where did the original story take place?

It took place about 1,500 years ago in China.

4. What are the major changes that Disney made to the original Mulan story?

- Clash with the traditional role of a woman.

- Matchmaking episode.
- Addition of guardian dragon Mushu, lucky pet Cri-Kee, admirer Li Shang, three funny fellow soldiers, and grandma.
- Details of setting fire on the Great Wall and fighting on Tiananmen to save the emperor.
- Omission of younger brother and older sister.
- Wounded in battle, discovered as woman, and discharged.
- Indication of marriage to Li Shang.

5. Why did Disney make these changes?

Disney is in show business. It has to consider the taste of viewers to sell its products. The values of western culture are quite different from those of eastern culture, so Disney made some adjustments to make the story more appropriate for a western audience. Thus the movie is more or less a westernized Chinese story. For example, in the movie, *Mulan* has to be discovered as a woman and banished for the story to appear more reasonable to western viewers; a dragon has to be added to make the movie look more Chinese because a dragon is a symbol of the Chinese culture.

6. How do you like the changes?

The changes may make the story amusing and entertaining. The changes also may make it less culturally accurate for a person with a Chinese background. For example, Chinese people regard dragons as their ancestors and respect them very much. They would not use a dragon as a pet, a guardian, or a source of laughter or entertainment.

Media Stereotype Detectors

Rationale

Stereotyping exists in programs that children watch. Because stereotyping presents children with fixed and conventional images of people, it leads them to false impressions of various groups of people. It affects the way children perceive others and the way they think and feel about themselves. Children need to learn how to recognize stereotypes, understand that data about groups do not tell them about individuals, and understand how media portrayals influence their ideas of members of society.

Objectives

- Students will understand that stereotypes exist in television and movies.
- Students will learn what stereotypes are, types of stereotypes, and techniques of stereotyping.
- Students will be able to recognize stereotypes.
- Students will see the impact of stereotypes.

Related Content Areas

- *Language arts:* Students will read and compare variations of folktales; use reading skills to comprehend elements of character development in literary works (for example, the differences between stereotypical characters and fully developed characters); write comparative descriptions of two images; and participate in discussions and activities.

- *Social studies:* Students will compare social groups and understand that culture influences people's identity, language, traditions, and behaviors. Students will also learn that although groups may act, hold beliefs, and present themselves as a cohesive whole, individual members may hold widely varying beliefs, so the behavior of groups or a culture may not be predictable from an understanding of their individual members. Students will enhance their appreciation of people of different cultural and ethnic backgrounds.

- *Fine arts:* Students will express ideas through art and show understanding of stereotypes through cartoon images and performance.

Preparation and Materials

- Set up a TV and VCR or DVD player and an overhead projector in the classroom.
- Bring in a copy each of the children's books *Amazing Grace*, by Hoffman (1991), and *Cinder Edna*, by Jackson (1998).
- Bring in copies of the Disney videos or DVDs *Cinderella, Snow White, Aristocats, Tarzan, Beauty and the Beast,* and *Home Alone.*
- Create a transparency of Learn About Stereotypes (page 84), or make copies as handouts for students.
- Make copies for students of Types of Stereotypes (page 85), Techniques for Stereotyping (page 86), and Viewing Guide for *Home Alone* (page 87) handouts.
- Estimated time for unit: 7 hours.

> ➤ **TIP**
>
> *You won't be showing the Disney movies, so you could bring in images of the movie covers or posters instead of the movies themselves.*

Procedure

1. To introduce the concept of stereotyping, display samples of children's movies: *Cinderella, Snow White, Tarzan, Beauty and the Beast,* and *Aristocats.* Point out that many Disney movies have princesses and princes or their equivalent female and male characters. Ask students what words they believe best describe the kinds of main characters in the movies on display. Brainstorm adjectives that describe princesses/females and princes/males. Adjectives in the following list may appear:

   Princess/female: beautiful, pretty, young, rich, lovely, delicate, graceful, lady-like, not very resourceful, helpless, and dependent on luck or magic to be saved.

   Prince/male: young, handsome, strong, rich, manly, versatile, smart, and loving.

   Point out to students that Disney movies have stereotyped females and males.

2. Read aloud the story *Cinder Edna,* then as a class, work on a Venn diagram on the board to see the differences and similarities of the stereotyped and the nonstereotyped Cinderella. (See page 77 for an example of a Venn diagram.)

3. Put the transparency Learn about Stereotypes on the overhead projector (or pass it out as a handout). Discuss the definition of a stereotype.

4. Discuss types of stereotypes and techniques for stereotyping. Give or invite students to give examples, then pass out the Types of Stereotypes and Techniques for Stereotyping handouts and discuss the topics further.

5. Students will next search the media for proof of stereotypes using the movie *Home Alone* as an example. Before showing the movie, brainstorm with students (and write on the board) words to describe

   - a nine-year-old boy
   - a villain
   - a big brother

6. Keep the notes on the board. Ask students if they have seen any of the *Home Alone* movies. Pass out the Viewing Guide for *Home Alone* handout and ask students to take notes and answer the questions while watching. Show part of the first *Home Alone.* (Be sure to include scenes that show Kevin, his brother, and the villains.)

7. Have students draw cartoon pictures of the characters to go with their descriptions and discuss the handout. Point out that stereotypes exist in media to affect our worldviews, and ask students to suggest other stereotypes that exist on television and in movies.

8. Divide the class into small groups and have each group work on one TV or movie image of stereotyped characters, such as a mother, a father, a grandmother, younger siblings, a stepmother, a teacher, or a Chinese, Jewish, or African American person. Have students write down words or phrases that describe the stereotyped character they've chosen. For example,

   Grandma: old and overweight, wearing glasses, walks unsteadily, stays at home, and loves grandchildren but does not understand why they dress, talk, and act the way they do.

9. Next, ask each student to pick one stereotyped image to compare with someone they know. Have each student write short descriptions of the two images, the stereotyped image and the real person. For example:
   "My grandma is different from the TV image because she is not old looking and does not wear glasses. She is fairly slim and energetic. She goes ballroom dancing every weekend. She buys me games for my Game Boy Advanced."

10. Discuss the dangers and impact of stereotyping on our lives. Ask questions from the Discussion Guide for Impact of Stereotypes (page 89) and use the answers on that guide as a reference for the discussion.

11. Read aloud *Amazing Grace* and discuss with students the potential opportunities for Grace when she refuses to fall into the stereotype trap. When classmates say Grace can't play Peter Pan in the school play because she is black and a girl, her mother and grandmother lovingly reaffirm all possibilities. Thus convinced, Grace wins the part, acting out a magical Peter Pan. At the tryouts, the class agrees that she is the best for Peter Pan. Ask students, "What if Grace fell for the stereotype? Would she have done what she did?"

Adaptations

- For lower elementary, special needs, or ESL students, instead of handing out Types of Stereotypes and Techniques for Stereotyping, you might teach only those terms that are appropriate for your students.

- Lower elementary, special needs, or ESL students could discuss the Viewing Guide to *Home Alone* questions together as a class instead of writing their own answers.
- Lower elementary, special needs, or ESL students could draw pictures or talk about the comparison between stereotyped images and a real person instead of writing descriptions.

Assessments

- Check student participation in successfully completing the Venn diagram.
- Check student understanding through completion of the Viewing Guide for *Home Alone*.
- Evaluate student descriptions for accurate comparison of the differences and similarities of a stereotyped character with a real person and for mechanical correctness.
- Evaluate student understanding through their active participation in class discussions and activities on stereotypes.

Learn About Stereotypes

Definition:

Stereotype refers to oversimplified generalizations about a group of people without consideration for individual differences. To label an entire group based on the actions of a few of them is stereotyping. Stereotypes use patterns of dress, physical characteristics, and behaviors that are easily recognized and understood. A positive or a negative judgment is often made about the person or group being stereotyped. Stereotypes are not realistic and are predictable.

For example: When people talk about specific nationalities, religions, races, or genders as "smart," "hard working," "cheap," "lazy," "criminal," or "dumb," they are expressing stereotypes.

Types of Stereotypes

People are stereotyped in media in many ways. Here are some examples of these ways.

Race or ethnicity: such as White, African American, Asian, Hispanic, Arabic, Jewish, Native American

For example: Asian Americans are depicted as successful model racial groups. African Americans are depicted as dangerous criminals. Jewish people are depicted as shrewd and greedy.

Nationality or culture: such as German, French, Irish, Italian, Chinese

For example: Math-smart Chinese are shown as good at cooking and gong fu. Irish people are shown to drink, sing, and argue a lot. Emotional Italians are depicted as loud people who talk with their hands. Germans are seen as intelligent and serious.

Sex: boys, girls, men, women

For example: Boys are supposed to play with cars and wear blue while girls play with Barbie and wear pink.

Men are shown as strong, tough (they never cry), in control, sporty, and adventurous, with important jobs, while women are depicted as nagging homemakers, delicate, passive, dependent, loving, and devoted.

Age: such as elderly, children, teenagers, babies

For example: Teenagers are often depicted as rebellious. Young kids are often shown as cute and smarter than adults. Elderly people are shown as weak, grouchy, and inflexible.

Profession: such as engineer, librarian, artist, professor, teacher, doctor, lawyer, cook, policeman, criminal

For example: Tough-looking policemen supposedly shoot at people, crash cars, and chase criminals but are often outwitted. Librarians supposedly are quiet, stern, single, and stuffy, and wear glasses.

Appearance: such as overweight, slim, skinny, beautiful, ugly, tall, short

For example: Short and skinny guys are often depicted as shrewd and cunning. Young, beautiful, tall, and slim women are often shown as dimwitted models.

Family members: such as husband, wife, grandma, grandpa, father, mother, big brothers and sisters, younger brothers and sisters

For example: Big brothers and sisters are usually shown as mean and unsympathetic. Little brothers and sisters are depicted as annoying and attention-getting. Often the loving and old-looking grandma bakes wonderful cookies.

Techniques for Stereotyping

Stereotyping in the media uses exaggeration of people's characteristics to build characters.

Examples of characteristics that can be exaggerated:

Physical characteristics

- Appearance: clownish, ugly, evil, sinister, beautiful, smart, tall, short, big, or skinny
- Dress: neat, pretty, handsome, shabby, old fashioned, ethnic, conservative, or progressive

For example: A Chinese man has slanted eyes and wears long gowns and pigtails.

Personalities: quick temper, shy, extrovert, introvert, quiet, talkative, loving, aggressive, or helpful

For example: Big ladies with a loving heart are talkative.

Speech manners: yelling, shouting, talking, chatting; using a loud, mean, sweet, foolish, smart, nice, serious, or humorous voice.

For example: A judge speaks in a serious and authoritarian voice. Professors talk in bookish and academic jargons (words no one else can understand).

Behaviors: foolish, smart, clumsy, mean, fast, or slow behaviors.

For example: Policemen always dash in wrong directions chasing criminals. Stepmothers treat stepdaughters meanly. Japanese women are obedient to their husbands.

Beliefs: certain colors or numbers are regarded as luckier than others; god or other supernatural being oversees us.

For example: Pocahontas consults Grandma Willow. Asian cultures regard red as lucky, gold as wealth, and blue as career success.

Attitudes: positive, negative, authoritarian, rebellious, serious, or humorous.

For example: A teenager daughter rebels by not following the curfew rule.

Viewing Guide for Home Alone

1. What types of characters do you see? List at least three.

   _____

   _____

   _____

2. What words or phrases best describe each of the characters?

   Villains: _____

   Kevin: _____

   Big brother: _____

3. Did the character's actions (behaviors) tell you something about him?
   Give examples.

   Villains: _____

   Kevin: _____

   Big brother: _____

4. Does the clothing suggest what kind of person the character might be? What
   are the characters dressed like?

   Villains: _____

   Kevin: _____

   Big brother: _____

5. Does the character's appearance tell you anything about him? How does the
   character look?

   Villains: _____

   Kevin: _____

   Big brother: _____

6. Does the way a character talks tell you anything about him? How do the characters talk?

   Villains: _____

   Kevin: _____

   Big brother: _____

7. Are the characters true to life or unrealistic?

   _____

8. Are the characters stereotypes?

   _____

9. Draw a cartoon picture of one of the characters based on your impression from the movie.

Discussion Guide for Impact of Stereotypes

Ask the following questions of students and guide them in discussion with the sample answers beneath each question.

1. What does being "manly" or "ladylike" mean in stereotypes?

   Manly means tough, unemotional, dominating, fixing cars, and so on.

   Ladylike means lovely, delicate, passive, gentle, cooking, sewing, and so on.

2. What names are men and women called if they do not fit into these roles?

   Men are called sissies, nerds, or wimps, and women are called tomboys.

3. Where do we learn gender stereotypes?

   From society, our community, our family, and media. We are not born this way; we learn our gender roles from society.

4. Why do TV and movies use stereotypes?

   Stereotypes enable viewers to understand a character's role quickly and easily. In short shows, when there isn't much time to develop characters fully, stereotypes are used for the convenience of creating easily understood characters and plots.

5. What are the impacts of stereotyping on us?

   Stereotypes confirm and tell us that we must perform certain roles in order to fit in. They take away our choices in determining what we want to do and be; limit our potential; and mislead us about and narrow our ways of looking at people or groups of people and ourselves. Stereotypes make us believe that all people belonging to certain groups behave in the same way. They present a distorted representation of society and lead us to make biased judgments about people. Negative stereotypes can lead to simplistic and dangerous "good versus evil," "bad guys versus good guys" perceptions.

3

Advertising Is Everywhere

Media create a fantasy world of materialistic lifestyles, with fashionable clothes, new appliances, and exotic vacations. With repeated messages, commercials encourage us to buy our way to happiness. Advertising is everywhere in our lives, informing us about new products and ideas, while it entertains us and supports the mass media industry. Advertising can be deceptive, however, and promotes consumerism at the expense of values such as thriftiness and conservation.

Every day, children are bombarded by advertising, urging them to buy certain products in order to be popular and fit in. Marketing to children may hurt their self-esteem and damage their values and worldviews. Is it possible to raise independent-minded children in this highly commercialized culture?

The units in this chapter are designed to help children understand the nature and goal of advertising, develop critical-thinking skills to understand and identify advertising techniques, take action, make responsible purchasing decisions, and learn that consumerism is not the way to happiness. The units are intended to help children become mature and informed consumers and citizens.

What Is Advertising?

Rationale

Children need to learn the basics of advertising–definition, types, and media where advertising appears–before we teach them critical skills for becoming mature consumers.

Objectives

- Students will be able to define advertising.
- Students will understand that the purpose of advertising is to sell products, ideas, or services.
- Students will identify advertising from different media and understand how advertising influences every aspect of media.

Related Content Areas

- **Language arts:** Students will participate in class discussions and in show and tell.
- **Fine arts:** Students will appreciate art, music, and humor in advertising.

Preparation and Materials

- Collect and display examples of advertising from different mass media: audiotapes and videos of ads from radio and TV; newspaper ads (such as photo ads, classified ads, shopping guides); magazine ads (such as fragrance strips and pop-up ads); ads on merchandise (such as backpacks with Harry Potter or Hello Kitty logos, T-shirts with Nike logos, and cereal boxes); catalogs; and pictures of billboards and electronic bulletin boards.
- Set up a TV and VCR, radio, and overhead projector in the classroom.
- Create a transparency of Advertising in Media (page 96) and Discussion Questions on Advertising (page 97) or make copies for students.
- Make copies for students of the Advertising in Our Lives handout (page 98).
- Estimated time for unit: 3 hours.

Procedure

1. With samples of advertising on display, begin the unit by humming one or two TV or radio jingles that you think your students might know. Ask volunteers to share a few more jingles that stand out in their minds.
2. Ask your students if they know what the songs are. If the words "advertising" or "commercial" come up, write them down on the board. As a class, brainstorm things the words "advertising" and "commercial" remind them of and write the answers on the board.
3. Talk about the major kinds of media that advertisers usually put their ads in, then display the transparency Advertising in Media (or pass out as a handout) to show further examples to students.
4. Display the transparency Discussion Questions on Advertising (or pass out as a handout) and have students discuss the questions and topics in small groups, and then open up the discussion to the entire class.
5. Try to come up with a class definition for advertising, making sure you include the following in some way:

   Advertising appears on TV, on radio, in newspapers, on billboards, on lunchboxes, on the Internet, and so on. Advertising tells people about products, ideas, and services and uses many techniques to persuade them to buy. The advertiser creates and pays for the ads to appear in media. Thus advertising supports media financially. Advertising influences every aspect of media: it sponsors programs, determines the structure of newspapers and scheduling of TV programs, and so on.

6. As homework, ask students to look around at home or in their neighborhood for examples of advertising. They should find at least five examples of advertising from different media and complete the Advertising in Our Lives handout by examining the ads, thinking about the messages, and identifying mass media that carry the ads.

7. Students present their homework in class.

Adaptations

You may choose to teach from the handout instead of giving it to children, depending on the age and reading level of your students.

Assessments

- Observe whether students can define advertising, recognize ads from different media, and identify the media carrying the ad.
- Evaluate accurate completion of the Advertising in Our Lives handout.
- Check student understanding through active participation and contributions in discussion.

> ➤ **TIP**
>
> *For extra credit, students could rewrite the words to popular jingles to form anti-advertising songs or songs that "sell" such things as good manners, healthy choices, and values.*

Is This Paradise or What?

Advertising in Media

All advertising sells various products and services, such as travel, cars, home appliances, toys, computers, and so on.

Print Media

Newspapers

International, national, and local newspapers carry advertising. For example, *USA Today*, the *Washington Post*, and the *New York Times* all carry advertising. Types of ads include shopping guides; Sunday supplements and circulars; display ads (which include copy, photos, illustrations, large type, and often coupons); and classified ads, which sell goods, services, and opportunities of all kinds, such as real estate, cars, employment, used items, yard sales, workers wanted, and so on.

Magazines

International, national, and local magazines carry advertising: For example, *TV Guide*, *Newsweek*, *Better Homes & Gardens*, *National Geographic*, *Woman's Day*, *Cosmopolitan*, and *Sports Illustrated* all carry advertising. Types of ads include display ads, pop-up ads, fragrance strips, makeup strips, insert cards (selling the magazine itself), and so on.

Electronic Media

TV

National and regional broadcast TV and cable TV carry ads. For example, CNN, USA network, the Discovery Channel, TBS, MTV, Fox Family, Nickelodeon, Disney, ABC, NBC, CBS, and so on all carry advertising.

Types of ads include commercials and infomercials for products, services, and ideas (such as political and community service ads), and commercials that advertise television programs.

Radio

Radio is a mobile and one-on-one medium, with national and local stations both carrying ads: For example, ABC Radio Networks, CBS Radio Networks, National Public Radio, and so forth all carry ads. Types of ads include commercials for products, services, and ideas, and commercials that advertise radio programs.

Internet

Websites are filled with ads. For example, Yahoo, MSN, Amazon, Ask Jeeves, and Walt Disney Internet Group all carry advertising. Types of ads include banner ads, clickable button ads, pop-up ads, classified ads, and e-mail ads selling products, services, and ideas.

Cellular Phones

Cell phones receive short message service (SMS) that advertises telecommunication services and other telephone-related services.

Outdoor

Outdoor advertising includes billboards and poster panels in subways and buses, electronic bulletins along busy highways, and large electronic screens along busy streets, all selling products, services, and ideas.

Direct Mail

Direct mail refers to ads you receive in the mail, such as postcards, sale-letters, circulars, coupon packets, and catalogs.

Discussion Questions on Advertising

- Tell the group about your favorite ads.

- Do you like watching ads on TV? Why or why not?

- Do you look at ads on the Internet? Do you like them?

- What do you think ads are trying to do?

- Who creates ads and who pays for them?

- Recall mass media or other places where you have seen ads.

- Why do you think ads appear in mass media?

- What are the pros and cons of ads being in media?

CLEARANCE

$49⁹⁹

Sing-A-Long Song
Sound System
with Microphone
Super Store

Advertising in Our Lives

Examine advertising to look for their messages (what the ads try to tell you) and to identify the media that carry them. In the special information section, write about anything unique in your examples.

	Ad Titles	Messages	Media	Special Information
1.				
2.				
3.				
4.				
5.				
6.				

Is This Paradise or What?

Make Your Own Decisions

Rationale

Children need to learn the important skill of assessing their real needs so that they can say no to advertisers trying to sell them things they do not need.

Objectives

- Students will learn to recognize the selling purpose and misleading nature of advertising.
- Students will learn self-discipline by identifying options and understanding personal wants versus needs.
- Students will learn to make purchasing decisions according to needs.

Related Content Areas

- **Language arts:** Students will role-play in class, share experiences, work orally, write critical essays about bad ads, and enter a bad ad contest (if in grade five or above).
- **Math:** Students will use addition and division (calculating average numbers).

Preparation and Materials

- Gather two or three products and ads that do not match each other. For example, cosmetics that promise to make people look fifteen years younger; weight-loss products that work only with a healthy diet and exercise; and cleaning products that promise to work without any scrubbing.
- Bring in something you bought just because it was on sale (something you didn't really need).
- Make copies for students of the Do I Really Need Them? (page 103) handout.
- Collect enough brand-name products and their associated ads for each pair of students to have one set. Choose items that are desirable to your students.
- Bookmark or add to the Favorites list on student computers the winning entries from last year's Bad Ad Contest, at http://www.nmmlp.org/activism.htm (click on BadAd Contest near the top of the page), or print out the entries for students to read.
- Estimated time for unit: 5 hours.

Procedure

1. Share with the class your examples of two or three ads and their advertised products that don't match up. Encourage students to see the differences between the descriptions given in the ads and the products themselves. For example:

   - A bag of slimming tea and its ad that claims, "You will shake off 25 pounds in seven days drinking this thousand-year-old and all natural slim tea." This ad is misleading because the fine print on it also says, "It must be accompanied by a healthy diet and exercise to achieve the best effect."
   - A soda cup from a fast food restaurant with a number covered by a small label and the ad, which says, "Collect all three numbers, 23, 45, and 87, and you will WIN a trip to Disneyland for three!" We all know that it is almost impossible to collect the numbers needed to win these sweepstakes. The astronomical odds of winning are only in the fine print.
   - The product and ad for a skin repair product, which says, "I'm ready for my close-up now. Sk-II reduced my fine lines in just two weeks. Using Repair C, I like what I see." The model on the clear skin ad is a twenty-year-old woman who does not have wrinkles on her face.

     Also share something you bought just because it was on sale even though you did not really need it.

2. Ask students to share experiences of buying something because it was on a TV commercial that they regretted buying later because they did not really need it or the product did not live up to their expectations.

3. Review definitions of advertising and its purposes and introduce the topic for this lesson. (For help with the review, see Unit 12.)

4. Pass out the Do I Really Need Them? handout and ask students to write in the lefthand column the last five items they bought. Invite volunteers to share their answers.

5. Have them fill out the next four columns, answering where they heard about the product and what the advertising claimed; whether the product matched the ads; whether it was a brand-name item; and what it cost.

6. Discuss which things on their list they could have done without and which are available from a generic or alternative brand that's less expensive. If they could have bought a less expensive brand, how much would that item have cost? Have them fill in these answers on the handout. Encourage students to think about whether they purchased an item because they needed it or because they wanted it for comfort, to feel good, or to impress others. Students may ask their parents for help with the cost of items if they don't know.

7. In the final column, students figure out how much they could have saved by buying a cheaper brand or by not buying the item at all. Have them add up the amounts in the last column to see how much they could have saved, then write that amount at the bottom of the handout.

> **➤ TIP**
>
> *Students in grade five or above can enter their critical essays in the Bad Ad Contest. See the guidelines at http://www.nmmlp. org/activism.htm (click on BadAd Contest near the top of the page).*

8. Have students share their total possible savings and write these numbers on the board. Write down the number of students in the class. Ask students to calculate the average amount that each student could have saved. (Review or teach the concept of average numbers if necessary.)

9. Ask students to pair up and pick one brand-name product from your samples. Pass out the Questions to Ask Before You Purchase handout and have pairs examine the products and practice asking and answering the questions orally.

10. As homework, students take the list of questions with them on a weekend shopping trip and use it before they buy anything. After the weekend, students share their experiences with the class.
11. To conclude the unit, have students look at the winning entries of the New Mexico Media Literacy Project's Bad Ad Contest at http://www.nmmlp.org/activism.htm (click on BadAd Contest near the top of the page). Invite students to work in groups and look for ads that are annoying, untruthful, misleading, and offensive and write critical essays about these bad ads.

Adaptations

- For lower elementary, special needs, or ESL students, you may omit calculating the average amount of money that each person could have saved and the critical essay.
- You may choose to teach from the handout instead of giving it to children, depending on the age and reading level of your students.

Assessments

- Observe student understanding through participation in the discussion of the misleading nature of advertising.
- Observe student understanding through participation in asking and answering questions for purchasing brand-name products and their work with the Questions to Ask Before You Purchase handout.
- Check that students get the correct amount that they could have saved, the correct total amount the class could have saved, and the correct average amount that each person in the class could have saved.
- Evaluate the critical essay for student understanding, fulfillment of requirements, and mechanical correctness.

Do I Really Need Them?

Product	Brand	Cost	Source of information about product	Ad claims	Does product match ads?	Reason for buying	Do you need it?	Is there a less expensive or generic brand available?	Cost of other brand?	Possible savings
New backpack	Harry Potter logo	$40	TV commercial	Kids fly wearing it	No, I didn't fly like Harry when wearing it.	Friends own. Love Harry.	No.	Yes (backpacks without Harry Potter logo).	$20	$20
Electronic dictionary	Panasonic	$99.99	Friends	Proficient in Spanish in one month	No, I learned some, but not proficient.	Has games, keeps time and phone numbers.	No.	Yes (non-electronic dictionary).	$10.99	$80

Your total possible savings: _____

The Media-Savvy Student © 2004 Zephyr Press, Chicago, IL • (800) 232-2187 • www.zephyrpress.com

Questions to Ask Before You Purchase

Do I really need the product?

_____

Can I do without it?

_____

Why do I need this particular brand?

_____

Will it make me happy and for how long?

_____

Can I use a generic or less expensive brand?

_____

In what ways is the product like the ads?

_____

In what ways is it different?

_____

Should I buy the product based on the ads?

_____

Jump on the Bandwagon?

Rationale

Advertisers use persuasive techniques to sell. It is crucial to introduce students to these techniques so that they will be able to detect hidden persuaders in advertising they encounter every day.

Objectives

- Students will learn to recognize persuasive techniques that are used to sell and will create advertising using these techniques.
- Students will practice public speaking and performing skills.

Related Content Areas

- *Language arts:* Students will recognize, understand, and communicate with persuasive writing devices; write short commercial scripts; and give a public speech.
- *Math:* Students will use percentages and compare two things using graphs.
- *Fine arts:* Students will use self-chosen styles and media to illustrate an idea and will perform commercials.

Preparation and Materials

- Videotape 12 commercials from television.
- Set up a TV and VCR in the classroom.
- Bring in a camcorder (optional).
- Make copies for students of Persuasive Techniques in Commercials (page 108) and Identify Hidden Persuaders in Ads (page 109) handouts.
- Provide art project supplies, such as poster board and markers.
- Provide thumbtacks or adhesive for displaying art projects.
- Estimated time for unit: 4 hours.

Procedure

1. Invite the class to look at the first two taped TV commercials together. Ask students:

    - What are the messages in the ads?
    - How do the ads try to sell you products?
    - Do the ads say that you will be special if you buy the products?
    - Do the ads tell you to hurry?

2. Pass out the Persuasive Techniques in Commercials handout. Explain that the handout lists some commonly used persuasive techniques in commercials. Go over the techniques one by one with students and illustrate with examples from commercials. Make sure everyone becomes familiar with the techniques. Give students some extra time to reflect if needed.

3. Have students work in small groups. Each group picks one persuasive technique to illustrate through an art project in whatever style and media they choose. Introduce styles of drawing (such as cartoon, realistic, naïve, and so forth) and different media (such as oil paint, chalk, markers, colored pencils, and so forth) if necessary. When students are finished, display the illustrations on a wall or bulletin board.

4. Pass out the Identify Hidden Persuaders in Ads handout and ask students to complete the handout while they watch the rest of the videotaped commercials twice. After viewing the tape, compare notes as a class to see if students identified the techniques correctly. Discuss how these techniques work in commercials.

5. Next, students create their own advertising using persuasive techniques. Have them work in small groups to compose ads to sell something to the class. Students may act out commercials or create illustrated ads with poster paper and markers. Videotape acted out commercials if possible.

6. Students present their commercials to the class. You might invite parents and students from other classes to attend.

7. As homework, ask students to watch a 30-minute TV program and keep track of the time the network spends broadcasting commercials. Have them calculate the percentage of time spent on commercials during this program, then draw a pie or bar graph to compare the time spent on commercials with the time spent on the program itself.

Adaptations

- For gifted, upper elementary, and middle school students, the lesson can be extended to include having students videotape their own commercials or use persuasive techniques to make speeches as political candidates.
- Lower elementary, special needs, or ESL students could learn to recognize persuasive techniques without creating their own commercials.
- You may choose to teach from the handouts instead of giving them to children, depending on the age and reading level of your students.

> **➤ TIP**
>
> *For extra credit, students could write a report on the different ways media could make money if they didn't sell advertising space.*

Assessments

- Evaluate student responses to the Identify Hidden Persuaders in Ads handout to see if students can correctly identify persuasive techniques from commercials.
- Check whether students show understanding of persuasive techniques through their illustrations.
- Observe whether students successfully create commercials using persuasive techniques.
- Evaluate student accuracy in tracking and calculating the percentage of time on commercials within a 30-minute program, and in illustrating the information in graphs.

Persuasive Techniques in Commercials

Bandwagon: Telling the audience that everyone is buying it, using it, or doing it, so they should join the crowd!
For example: "Are you the only one in the neighborhood who does not have a Game Boy Advanced?"

Testimonial: Using a famous person or an authority to promote products.
For example: Michael Jordan says, "Do you know what helps me win? Two glasses of Cowed Milk a day!"

Transfer: Transferring the audience's positive feelings about something or someone to the product.
For example: "If you like Harry Potter, you will love the Harry Potter candy bar."

Repetition: Saying something again and again so people will remember it.
For example: "It is hot, hot, hot!" "It is free! No charges to your credit card."

Name-calling: Making a product seem better by saying derogatory things about its competition. For example: "Other homework helpers just want to take your money while we really help you get A's."

People just like you: Using an ordinary or average person who represents the audience to sell the product or service, implying that you are alike, and if this person would use, buy, or believe this, you should, too.
For example: "If you are an allergy sufferer like me, use Aqueous Nasal Spray. Spray it and breathe in. You are back to yourself! If it helps me, it'll help you."

Call for Action: Making you feel that you have to do something immediately or the opportunity will be lost forever.
For example: "Friday night only! Better hurry! Only a limited supply is available."

Flag Waving: Connecting the person, idea, or product with patriotism, implying that you are unpatriotic if you don't buy the product or service or believe the idea.
For example: "I am a patriotic American. I visit McDonald's no matter which country I am in."

Identify Hidden Persuaders in Ads

Watch the commercials and try to identify each persuasive technique used in them.

Technique	Bandwagon	Evidence
Bandwagon	Yes No	
Testimonial	Yes No	
Transfer	Yes No	
Repetition	Yes No	
Name-calling	Yes No	
Just like you	Yes No	
Call for Action	Yes No	
Flag Waving	Yes No	

Find Out for Yourself

Rationale

Hands-on science experiments enable children to see for themselves how truthful advertising is by testing the advertisers' claims.

Objectives

- Students will become critical about advertising and not take the scientific claims at face value.
- Students will test ad truth through their own scientific experiments.
- Students will use writing to make a change in society.

Related Content Areas

- ***Language arts:*** Students will practice problem solving; scientific note taking; formal letter writing; composition of a well-organized science report; and speaking and listening through discussion and oral presentation.
- ***Science:*** Students will use scientific inquiry to investigate questions, conduct experiments, and solve problems.
- ***Math:*** Students will practice figuring percentages, creating graphs, and using the mathematical results in writing.
- ***Fine arts:*** Students will artfully display experiment results on a bulletin board.

Preparation and Materials

- Videotape several TV commercials that base their claims on experiments, such as dishwashing liquid that fights grease, kills germs, and shines; washing detergent that cleans the toughest stains; toothpaste that whitens teeth; lotion that corrects wrinkles, dark circles, and puffy eyes, and so forth.
- Purchase one of the products shown on the videotape. For example, you could test a detergent that supposedly "fights the toughest stains with a single wash."
- Send a letter to parents before beginning the unit explaining that students will need to purchase a product shown in commercials for the purpose of an in-class experiment. Include a list of products in the letter (those products that match the commercials you plan to show in class). Note that students will be working in small groups and need only one product per group.
- Make copies for students of the Viewing Log for TV Commercials (page 113) and Truthful or Not? (page 114) handouts.
- Prepare tables, counters, or other areas for student experiments.
- Clear a bulletin board area for display.
- Estimated time for unit: 5 hours.

Procedure

1. To begin the unit, students watch the videotaped TV commercials together. Ask the class if they notice anything these ads have in common. Lead them to the conclusion that they all base their claims on some kind of experiment.
2. Pass out the Viewing Log for TV Commercials handout. Play the video again and ask the students to take notes on the products advertised, the claims, and the kinds of experiments the claims are based on.
3. Demonstrate how to duplicate an experiment with one product to see how well the product matches the claims. Encourage students to take notes on the experiment.
4. Ask students to work in small groups to pick a product from the videotaped commercials. Ask students to bring in the product for the next day, as well as any materials they may need to conduct the experiment. Discuss the chosen products to make sure the experiments will be feasible and to see if you have materials in the classroom that students may use in their experiments.
5. The next day, students duplicate the experiments from the ads for the products they've chosen to find out if the claims are truthful or not. Teach or review how to document an experiment, including the observation (what

the product claims), the hypothesis (a guess about whether the claim will prove true), the steps of the experiment (including amounts of the product used, times, and other materials used), and the results.

6. Once the experiments are done, ask each group to write a brief report to document the experiment step by step and share the reports with the class.

7. Teach or review formal letter writing. Have students write to the manufacturers of their products explaining the results of their experiments. Have students work through the writing process in small groups (drafting, editing, and revising) before sending the letters out.

8. As a class, discuss the results of the experiments together and calculate the percentage of truthfulness in commercials on the Truthful or Not? handout. Have students write a report about truth in advertising, including graphs to show the results of the study.

9. Display the reports on a bulletin board or at a science fair. Encourage students to be artistic in displaying their reports. You might also send student reports to a local newspaper.

> **TIP**

Have students conduct their experiments at home with parents instead of in class with their small groups to get parents involved (and to save on class time and materials).

Adaptations

- For lower elementary, special needs, or ESL students, an experiment can be done as a whole class with teacher guidance. The class may work on the same topic and write one report together.

- You may choose to teach from the handouts instead of giving them to children, depending on the age and reading level of your students.

- Gifted, upper elementary, and middle school students may choose their own commercials and products from TV, radio, newspapers, magazines, and so forth.

Assessments

- Observe whether students can duplicate an experiment accurately, with an understanding of the scientific process.

- Observe students' ability to critically evaluate the truthfulness of the claims.

- Evaluate the letters and reports for accuracy, completeness, and mechanical correctness.

- Check the accuracy of student percentage calculations and graphs.

Name _____

Viewing Log for TV Commercials

Watch the commercials and describe the products being advertised, the claims made, and the experiments the claims are based on.

Products	Advertised Claims	Experiments

Truthful or Not?

For each experiment done in class, write a description of the ad and whether or not student experiments proved it to be truthful, not truthful, or in between. Then count up the total number of ads examined and the number of ads that fit into each truthfulness category. Calculate the percentage of truthful ads, untruthful ads, and in-between ads.

Ads	Truthful	Not Truthful	In Between

Total number of ads examined: _____

Number of ads in each category: _____

Truthful: _____

Not Truthful: _____

In Between: _____

Percentages of each category: _____

Truthful: _____

Not Truthful: _____

In Between: _____

4

Internet-Savvy Kids

Millions of children are online every day. The interactive nature of the Internet empowers children by offering them opportunities for self-expression, communication, and education. We want children to benefit from the wealth of opportunity the Internet offers; however, we worry about letting them loose in cyberspace because there are dangers out there just as there are dangers in the real world. Children can interact with anyone online from home, school, or the library. The Internet allows any user, anywhere, to post any information, including materials that are inaccurate, misleading, and inappropriate for children. The friendly voice in a chat room could belong to someone with whom we don't want our children speaking. An innocent misspelling of a request on an Internet search engine could bring up a long list of links to sites that promote hate or violence, deliver adult content, or provide easy access to other sites that are inappropriate for children.

How are we going to deal with the dangers? Do we legislate or educate?

We suggest dealing with these dangers by educating our children about the Internet. We can give them guidelines and help them understand the basic open and nonprivate nature of the Internet and develop critical-thinking skills to recognize hate propaganda, protect themselves from online marketing, protect their personal privacy, learn proper Internet behavior, and search for quality information. This unit will introduce the Internet world to young children and help them develop skills for surfing critically so that they can use the Internet as a tool for life-long learning.

Safe Surfing

Rationale

The world of the Web is fascinating to children because of its lively and change-able nature. There are endless possibilities for fun, games, educational tools, and conversations with friends from all over the world. But the Internet has its dark side, too. Children need to be aware of the risks involved in surfing the Net, send-ing e-mails, and chatting online, and to learn critical skills so they will have safe and enjoyable Internet experiences.

Objectives

- Students will recognize the benefits and risks involved in online experiences.
- Students will create safe-surfing guidelines.
- Students will learn what to do when risks appear.

Related Content Areas

- **Language arts:** Students will compose rules for specific purposes and read and take notes on specific information online.
- **Fine arts:** Students will create a poster of safety rules.

Preparation and Materials

- Make copies for students of the Internet Safe-Surfing Pretest (page 120).
- Provide poster board and markers.
- Bookmark or add to the Favorites list on student computers the online article by Magid (1998), "Child Safety on the Information Highway," available at http://www.safekids.com/child_safety.htm, or print out copies for students.
- Review the following online articles and Web sites about Internet safety:
  "Don't Let the Web Catch You":
  http://www.thinkquest.org/library/site_sum.html?lib_id=2607&team_id=5210
  Kid Safety on the Internet Web site:
  http://www.ou.edu/oupd/kidsafe/start.htm
  Web Wise Kids Web site: http://www.webwisekids.com/
- Provide computers with Internet access, enough for each pair of students, if possible.
- Download to all classroom computers the online game Privacy Playground: The First Adventure of the Three Little CyberPigs, available at http://www.media-awareness.ca/english/special_initiatives/games/privacy_playground/index.cfm
- Be sure to play the Privacy Playground game yourself so that you are familiar with the game and can answer student questions.
- Estimated time for unit: 4 hours.

Procedure

1. Start the discussion by asking students to take a pretest about their knowledge of safe surfing and their home environment. Pass out the Internet Safe-Surfing Pretest. Have volunteers share their answers when everyone has completed the pretest.

2. Have students work in pairs to read "Child Safety on the Information Highway." Together, they locate and take notes on the risks involved in Internet communication, such as in chat rooms, e-mail, instant messaging, and online clubs.

3. Work with the whole class to brainstorm benefits and risks of the World Wide Web, e-mail, and chat rooms. Invite students to share personal experiences. Use the Discussion Guide on Internet Benefits and Risks (page 121) as a reference.

> ➤ TIP
>
> *If you have only one computer in the classroom, spread this unit out to give students time to take turns playing the Privacy Playground game.*

4. Discuss the question, "Can we imagine life without the Internet?" As a class, list things that we have access to and do with the Internet and the things that we would not be able to have or do without it. Write student answers on the board. Then ask follow-up questions:

   - What should we do with the Internet now that we are aware of all the risks involved?
   - Should we keep away from it? Why or why not?

   Try to come to the understanding that we should learn to use the Internet critically and properly. To do this, we can make and follow rules to avoid risks.

5. Have students get into small groups. Pass out poster board and markers to each group. Working in their groups, students discuss and make up rules that they think will protect them from online risks, creating a group poster of these rules. Use Sample Rules for Net Safe Kids (page 122) as a reference in helping students brainstorm rules.

6. As a class, agree on one version of the rules and create a new poster to hang on the wall. Ask students to write the rules down on a piece of paper to take home.

7. To conclude the lesson, invite students to play the game Privacy Playground: The First Adventure of the Three Little CyberPigs.

Adaptations

- For lower elementary, special needs, or ESL students, you may want to summarize the risks listed in Magid's article for them.
- You may choose to teach from the handouts instead of giving them to children, depending on the age and reading level of your students.
- If appropriate for your students, give more guidance in making up the safe-surfing rules.

Assessments

- Check student understanding in the notes they take after reading "Child Safety on the Information Highway."
- Evaluate student understanding from participation in class discussion.
- Evaluate student understanding in the posters they create.

Internet Safe-Surfing Pretest

1. Do you have access to the Internet at home? Do you use the Internet at home? _____

2. How much time do you spend online every day? _____

3. Do you finish homework and other chores before you go online?

   _____

4. What do you usually use the Internet for? Check all the relevant areas:
   ☐ research for school; ☐ games; ☐ e-mail; ☐ chat rooms; ☐ instant messaging; ☐ ICQ; ☐ shopping; ☐ other (list below):

   _____

5. Do you have family rules for online use at home? _____

   _____

6. Are you concerned about Internet privacy? _____

   _____

7. Have you ever been asked to fill out a questionnaire to be eligible for a prize, to play a game, or to join a special club? Did you give any information? _____

   _____

8. Have you heard of or experienced anything negative or scary online, such as having a password stolen, a credit card stolen, identity stolen, or kids being harmed? _____

9. List the benefits and risks of

   e-mail: _____

   surfing the Internet: _____

   chat rooms: _____

Discussion Guide on Internet Benefits and Risks

Surfing the Internet

Benefits: Access rich educational and cultural resources; get help for homework; obtain up-to-the-minute information; improve ability to understand and evaluate information; access school Web sites; play fun games; learn skills useful for a future job.

Risks: Encounter age-inappropriate images and texts; encounter sites promoting hatred, violence, or drugs; encounter inaccurate, misleading, and untrue information; encounter commercials for alcohol and tobacco; encounter collectors of personal information from children; access games with excessive violence and gender stereotypes.

E-mail

Benefits: Keep in touch with teachers, family, and friends; get help for homework; practice writing; receive online newsletters; meet pen pals all over the world; learn foreign languages.

Risks: Talk to strangers; get uninvited e-mails about sites with adult materials, products for sale, or moneymaking methods.

Chat Rooms

Benefits: Make friends with children around the world; talk to children with similar interests and concerns in rooms designed for children and monitored by adults; communicate instantaneously with family, friends, and teachers.

Risks: Encounter offensive language and adult conversations; get to know and meet people who want to harm children; spend too much time online, ignoring friends, schoolwork, sports, and other people and activities.

Sample Rules for Net Safe Kids

- Stay away from Internet strangers the way you stay away from strangers on the street.

- Never tell anyone online that you are home alone.

- Never give your real last name, address, or telephone number to anyone online. If anyone asks for this information (or for your password), don't respond. Log off and tell your parents or teachers.

- If anyone uses nasty or mean language, do not respond. Log off right away. Report to parents or teachers right away if any information makes you feel uncomfortable.

- Never meet anyone in person that you have "met" online.

- Never send anyone your picture or anything else without first checking with your parents or teachers.

- Never accept anything from strangers, even if it is offered for free.

- Make up rules at home with your parents about what time of day you may go online, length of time you may spend online, and sites you may visit.

- Never make any online purchases without your parents' permission.

- Only visit kid-appropriate sites. If you find yourself in an "adults only" place on the Net, or anywhere you think you shouldn't be, log off!

Coping with an Avalanche of Information

Rationale

The sheer volume of information on the Web can be paralyzing, and being able to distinguish among fact, opinion, rumors, and lies is an important skill for Web surfers. The Internet is a useful resource for children, but there are poorly constructed sites with inaccurate and inappropriate information as well as informative and appropriate sites. Students need critical-thinking skills to locate quality, factual, and age-appropriate materials.

Objectives

- Students will understand that poorly constructed and inaccurate Web sites exist.
- Students will identify criteria for sound information.
- Students will practice locating quality, factual, and age-appropriate material.

Related Content Areas

Language arts: Students will compare information; use critical-reading skills; use a variety of criteria to evaluate the clarity and accuracy of information; and practice speaking and listening skills in discussion and presentation.

Preparation and Materials

- Make copies for students of the Web Site Evaluation Guide (page 127) and Will You Recommend This Web Site? (page 128) handouts.
- Provide computers with Internet access for each pair of students, if possible.
- Set up a classroom computer for all students to see. If possible, connect the computer to an overhead projector to enlarge the screen.
- Choose a simple topic you have accurate information about from a reliable source, such as water or polar bears. Have the information on hand.
- Find and bookmark or add to your Favorites list examples of Web sites on a topic of your choice that range from reliable to completely unreliable.
- Review the online article by Amit (2002), "How Do I Know When a Web Site is Good?" at http://www.acsd.k12.ca.us/tlc/library/howtouseweb.html#webeval.
- Estimated time for unit: 2 hours.

Procedure

1. Set up your computer so that all students can see the screen, and then go online. To introduce the topic, ask students to recall if they have ever tried to look for information on the Internet, typed in a keyword in a search engine, and been overwhelmed by what they found there. Demonstrate by typing in the word "rainforest," "deserts," or "oceans," and see how many Web sites you find.

2. Next, ask students if they have ever spent an entire hour online browsing and surfing and forgot why they went online or what they were looking for in the first place. Ask why they think this happens.

   Lead students to the understanding that the Internet is full of information on every topic. The volume of the information can be overwhelming and distracting for young students. One can never exhaust the information online, and some of this information is more reliable than other information. We need to learn critical-surfing skills to get to the best, most appropriate, and most reliable information.

3. Ask students' opinions about the statement: "If it is on the Internet, it must be true." Have an open discussion.

4. Write on the board a topic, such as water or polar bears. Ask students to write down what they know about it while you write down your information about the topic from a reliable source.

5. Ask volunteers to share their answers with the class, and then share your information and indicate the source of the information. Invite students to think about how accurate and reliable the information they have about the topic is. Point out that some information may be more reliable than other information.

6. Discuss what students think would happen if they put their information about water or polar bears on the Internet, as it is, without checking it against any sources. Ask them to rethink the statement, "If it is on the Internet, it must be true." Can they prove it or disprove it?

   Lead students to the understanding that anyone who can make a Web page can publish something on the Internet. Explain the difference between online and traditional publishing: traditional publishing goes through a series of "gatekeepers," such as editors, proofreaders, and fact checkers. On the Internet, authors can bypass these gatekeepers. As long as a person knows how to create a Web page, he or she can publish online, so there is no guarantee that all information online is true. We need to learn to analyze information on the Internet critically in order to find factual and accurate information. When we look for information on the Web, we have to evaluate the site to make sure we can trust the information on it.

7. Ask the class to brainstorm answers to the following questions:

   - How do we know when a Web site is good?
   - What should we consider to make sure the information is accurate and the site is appropriate?

   Suggest that students find out the following information about a site:

   Who—Who is the owner of the site (source of information and authority of that source)?

   What—Is the information objective and factual? Does it cover many perspectives?

   Appropriateness—Is the information age-appropriate (appealing to children and understandable to children)? Does the site make you feel uncomfortable in any way?

   When—Is the information updated and accessible?

8. Before sending children online to evaluate Web sites, review the definitions of fact and opinion. Explain that both facts and opinions exist on the Internet just as they do in other mass media.

9. Pass out and go over the Web Site Evaluation Guide with students. Use examples from Web sites to illustrate your points. For example, show students how to locate the author or contact information on a Web page, and where to find dates for when the information was copyrighted and last updated. Open several Web pages on a certain topic and illustrate how to choose the one that is more appropriate and reliable according to the guidelines in the handout.

10. Pass out the Will You Recommend This Web Site? handout and go over it with the class. Discuss the importance of each item. Have students work in pairs on computers to evaluate one Web site using the handout.

11. Have students share their evaluations of Web sites with their peers.

> ➤ **TIP**
>
> *If you don't have enough computers for students in your classroom, have them evaluate Web sites as homework or do the evaluation as a class. For young students, you might choose to evaluate the sites as a class regardless of your computer situation.*

Adaptations

- Choose age-appropriate topics for step 4, for your Web site examples, and for sites that your students are interested in analyzing.
- You may choose to teach from the handouts instead of giving them to children, depending on the age and reading level of your students.

Assessments

- Observe in discussions and activities to see if students understand the nature of information on the Internet.
- Check accurate completion of the Will You Recommend This Web Site? handout.

Web Site Evaluation Guide

Who created the Web site? Because anyone can make a Web page, there are unofficial sites and incorrect information online. You should look for information about who makes the site, such as an e-mail address, phone number, mailing address, or name. If you find information about the author, think about if he or she is an authority or expert on the topic or belongs to any organizations that you can trust. If you cannot find any contact information about the author of the site, use another site.

Is the information accurate and factual? Does it present many points of view? Some Web sites present one person's perspective or biased information, while others present several points of view with factual, detailed, and accurate information. If the Web site sounds biased and opinionated, or if you find only one point of view, go to another site.

When was it last updated? Look for a "last updated" date at the top or bottom of the homepage. If a site has been updated recently, it means someone is taking care of it and making sure that the information stays current. This date is not the same as a copyright date, which doesn't necessarily mean the site has or has not been updated.

Is the site easy to use and understand? If you cannot understand the site, look for another site. If the links come up very slowly, go to another one. Use your judgment.

Does the site have bad grammar or misspelled words? Knowing that anyone can make a Web site, bad spelling and poor grammar should make you wonder if the information is reliable. Most educated and responsible people use grammar fairly well and check their work for spelling errors, or have someone else do so. Watch out for sites that are full of errors.

Is the site age-appropriate? There are sites made just for adults. If you feel the site is not made for children, move on to another one. Use your judgment.

How do you learn about the site? Try to use Web sites that teachers and librarians recommend. Often they have links that have already been evaluated for quality and accuracy.

Will You Recommend This Web Site?

Name of Student: _____

Web Site: _____

Recommend it: _____ Don't recommend it: _____

Why or Why not? _____

_____

Accessibility

Is it easy to open the site? Does the link work? _____

Who

Who is the source of the information? Who created the Web site? Can you find this information?

_____

_____

Is the author an expert on the topic? What is the author's contact information?

_____

Does the author belong to an organization, a university, a research institution, or an agency that may add credibility to the site? _____

What

Is the information objective and factual or biased and opinionated?

_____

What viewpoints are presented? _____

_____

Is the information about the topic adequate for you? Do you need to look for more information on other sites? _____

Are there grammar or spelling errors in the writing? _____

When

Is the information up to date? Created or updated within the past two years?

_____

When was the Web site created? When was the Web site last updated?

_____

Appropriateness

Can you understand the information easily? _____

Does it look like a site made for children or for adults? _____

Is it fun to use? _____

Does the site appeal to you with colors and images? _____

Does the site make you feel uncomfortable in any way? _____

Netiquette

Rationale

Internet, or network, etiquette refers to proper behavior on the Internet, or the rules of cyberspace manners. It is very important for students to learn and follow the widely accepted rules of behavior on the Internet. Students should learn to use their very best manners online, just as they would at home or at school.

Objectives

- Students will learn proper behavior on the Internet and its importance.
- Students will identify netiquette rules.

Related Content Areas

- **Language arts:** Students will use reading and writing skills to make a difference: making up rules and composing a newsletter, a pamphlet, poetry, a bookmark, or a script.
- **Fine arts:** Students will show understanding and influence others through dramatic plays and art projects.

Preparation and Materials

- Bookmark or add to the Favorites list on student computers Disney Online's CyberNetiquette Comix "Mr. J. Thaddeus Toad in Web Mania," Episode 3, available at http://disney.go.com:80/family/webmania/.
- Be sure to play the Disney interactive comic first so that you are familiar with the content and can answer student questions.
- Review background information on netiquette for teachers: http://www.amit.org.il/learning/english/netiquette/ http://www.kidsdomain.com/brain/computer/surfing/netiquette_kids.html.
- Make copies for students of Netiquette Terms (page 132) and Netiquette to Remember Online (page 133) handouts.
- Estimated time for unit: 6 hours.

Procedure

1. Explain to students that they are going to learn proper and acceptable behavior on the Internet. As an introduction, give students some time to play the interactive comic game "Mr. J. Thaddeus Toad in Web Mania, Episode 3."

2. When the game is over, facilitate a discussion on netiquette. Ask students:
   - Do you think it is important to have good manners and to be polite to people? Why or why not?
   - What does Mr. Toad do that gets him in trouble? (List students' answers on the board.)
   - What is netiquette? Why is it so important?
   - What is spam?
   - Have you ever had chain letters sent to you? What should you do when you receive chain letters?
   - What is flaming? Have you experienced flaming? Share your experience with us.
   - How should you avoid online fighting?
   - Have you ever experienced yelling or shouting using all big letters in e-mails?

3. Give each student a copy of Netiquette Terms. Go over the terms with them. Use examples to illustrate the terms.

4. Hand out and go over Netiquette to Remember Online to prepare students for the next activity.

> ➤ **TIP**
>
> *If classroom computers are limited, play the Disney game as a class. Hook up your computer to an overhead projector, if possible, to enlarge the screen.*

5. Ask students to work in small groups and draw up a list of five do's and five don'ts that they consider to be most important for good netiquette. Students may use Netiquette to Remember Online as a guide. You might use Do's and Don'ts of Netiquette Sample Answers (page 156) as a guide to helping students think of and evaluate their ideas.

6. Start a class or school netiquette campaign. Students work in small groups to research information about netiquette using various resources, and then present their information in a variety of ways to help everyone understand and see the importance of netiquette. Students' projects should include information that answers the following questions:
   - What is netiquette?
   - Why is it important to be good netizens?
   - What are some examples of proper and improper behaviors on the Internet? Students could present their information in any or all of the following ways:
   - Publish a class newsletter on netiquette.
   - Make a pamphlet of netiquette to circulate.
   - Write and perform a dramatic play on netiquette.
   - Write poetry on netiquette, with illustrations.
   - Make posters about good netiquette
   - Make bookmarks of good netizens.

7. Invite parents or students from other classes to attend the presentation of the campaign.

Adaptations

- Lower elementary, special needs, or ESL students could do a poster or draw a bookmark about netiquette as a final project for the lesson; invite them to attend other students' campaign presentations, if possible.
- You may choose to teach from the handouts instead of giving them to children, depending on the age and reading level of your students.

Assessments

- Check for understanding and comprehension from scores in the Disney game.
- Check for understanding and comprehension of netiquette in the student lists of do's and don'ts of netiquette.
- Evaluate campaign projects to ensure that they cover the required information and effectively make other students aware of the issue.

Netiquette Terms

Capital letters: Using all capital letters in e-mails is equal to yelling or shouting at people in conversation.

Emoticons: These are symbols that people use in e-mails and chat rooms to show their moods. For example :-) means I am happy. :-(means I am sad. There are hundreds of these symbols used online.

Flaming: This refers to telling someone off online, which can lead to online fighting. It can occur in newsgroups, on Web forums, or in e-mails sent to many people.

Netiquette: Internet etiquette means behaving properly on the Internet. Netiquette is the collection of rules of cyberspace manners. It is very important to follow the accepted rules and be on your best behavior online.

Netizen: This term means "Net citizen." We should try to be good netizens on the Internet just as we are good citizens in society.

Newbie: A newbie is a new user of the Internet or of computers. We should be patient with all newbies.

Spam: Spam includes junk mail and chain letters on the Internet. It is similar to unsolicited marketing phone calls we receive. It is inappropriate netiquette to send or forward spam to people.

Netiquette to Remember Online

- Remember to be polite and courteous all the time. You are talking to people, not machines. Never begin e-mails without greetings and never end e-mails without telling people who you are.

- Remember privacy issues. You may create an online name (or pen name) to use online.

- Remember not to use all capital letters for emphasis online, because BIG LETTERS REPRESENT SHOUTING AND YELLING AT PEOPLE.

- Remember not to use rude and offensive language online; online providers will terminate your account if you do.

- Remember to avoid flame wars. Flaming is bad manners and can get out of control. Never flame others. If you are flamed, do not respond. Let your parents or teacher know.

- Remember to check your e-mails frequently and respond as soon as you can.

- Remember not to send personal messages to an entire newsgroup and remember to be brief to save time and space.

- Remember to use emoticons. Body language, facial expressions, gestures, and tones of voice are lost in online communication, and visual clues like entertaining emoticons in e-mails can help to prevent confusion :-). Avoid replacing words with emoticons, however, in case the other person is unfamiliar with what they mean. Also avoid them in formal writings.

- Remember to check your spelling and grammar before you send your e-mails.

- Remember to obey laws online the way you do offline. If it is against the law in the real world, it is against the law in the virtual world.

Recognizing Cyberad Strategies

Rationale

The Internet has become an attractive medium for advertisers who target children because of children's spending power, enthusiasm for the Internet, and tendency to accept information at face value. Online advertisers use many methods to get children to buy their products. They blend advertising with activities and games on the Internet so that children are being sold to without realizing it. It is crucial that we teach children how to recognize online commercial strategies so that they can be critical Internet users and consumers.

Objectives

- Students will learn to recognize online marketing strategies that target children.
- Students will become sensitive to online privacy issues.

Related Content Areas

- **Language arts:** Students will apply knowledge of language to critique and discuss online content; read and retell a story to enhance comprehension;

compose poems with personification; and express opinions and share experiences in discussion.

- **Math:** Students will understand money in terms of price and payment.
- **Fine arts:** Students will illustrate poems and make a bulletin board of poems.

Preparation and Materials

- Download to all classroom computers the online game Privacy Playground: The First Adventure of the Three Little CyberPigs, available at http://www.media-awareness.ca/english/special_initiatives/games/privacy_ playground/index.cfm.
- Be sure to play the Privacy Playground game yourself so that you are familiar with the game and can answer student questions.
- Set up a computer with Internet access for you to use in demonstrations for the class. For large classes, a computer hooked up to an overhead projector is effective. On your computer and on student computers, bookmark or add to the Favorites list a few commercial Web sites that sell to children under the guise of activities and games. For example:

    Disney Online:
    http://disney.go.com/park/homepage/today/flash/index.html

    HarryPotterFans.com: http://www.harrypotterfans.com/

    Yahooligans: http://www.yahooligans.com

    Pokemon World: http://www.pokemon.com

    The Cartoon Network: http://www.cartoonnetwork.com

    World Village: www.worldvillage.com

    DiscoveryKids.Com: http://kids.discovery.com/

- Make copies for students of the CyberPigs Comprehension Exercise (page 138), Strategies of Cyberads that Target Children (page 139), and Cyberad Scavenger Hunt (page 142).
- Create a transparency out of Cyberad Poems with Personification (page 143), or make copies as handouts for all students.
- Prepare bulletin board space to display student poems and provide materials for decorating the bulletin board, such as construction paper, markers, staplers, and scissors.
- Estimated time for unit: 4 hours.

> ➤ **TIP**
>
> *Try printing out examples of cyberads and Web sites in general for students to use when decorating the bulletin board.*

Procedure

1. Tell students that they are going to learn how to identify online advertising. Begin by reviewing what advertising is—messages that give people information about products or services with the purpose of selling those products or services.

2. Ask students the following questions and discuss their answers:

   - Have you encountered any online advertising before?
   - What kinds of advertising have you noticed online?
   - Has anyone ever bought something for you from online? Who?
   - What did this person buy for you? Was it a good experience? Why or why not?

3. Have students play the game Privacy Playground: The First Adventure of the Three Little CyberPigs as a pretest for the unit. If you have enough computers, have students play in pairs; alternatively, you could play the game as a class using one classroom computer. As they play the game, students should complete the CyberPigs Comprehension Exercise.

4. Ask students to retell the story of the Three Little CyberPigs in small groups and share the answers they put on the comprehension worksheet. Through open discussion, guide students to the following conclusions: Advertisers use many ways to sell things to children. Sometimes when we play online games, solve puzzles, interact with our favorite characters, and do other cool activities, we get advertising messages without realizing it. Often when we answer game questions, we are providing companies with marketing information. We should not take anything online at face value.

5. Using the Strategies of Cyberads handout as a guide, go online and show students some examples of ads and activities blended with ads.

6. Ask students to work in groups of five on a Web site scavenger hunt for ads and activities or games with marketing purposes. Give each student a copy of the Cyberad Scavenger Hunt, and have students fill out one worksheet for each Web site below. Provide students with the following commercial children's Web sites:

   HarryPotterFans.com: http://www.harrypotterfans.com/
   Yahooligans: http://www.yahooligans.com
   Pokemon World: http://www.pokemon.com
   The Cartoon Network: http://www.cartoonnetwork.com
   World Village: www.worldvillage.com

7. Have students share the online ads they identify from the Web sites and prepare short reports with information about the audience for the site, the strategies the Web site uses, and why these strategies are used.

8. For the next activity, teach or review what personification is. Explain to students that personification means giving thoughts and feelings to things that do not normally have any. Tell students that they will compose poems about cyberads and what we should do about them. For an example, use Cyberad Poems with Personification as a handout or transparency.

9. Students write drafts of their poems, then revise and illustrate them. Each student's poem should use personification to show his or her views, attitudes, and feelings about cyberads.

10. Guide the class in creating and decorating a bulletin board to display student poems.

Adaptations

- For lower elementary, special needs, or ESL students, steps 5 and 6 may be left out. They could do a dramatic play of the story the Three Little CyberPigs.
- You may choose to teach from the handouts instead of giving them to children, depending on the age and reading level of your students.

Assessments

- Check scores for the game the Three Little CyberPigs and completion of the CyberPigs Comprehension Exercise (see the list of possible answers on page 156 as a guide).
- Assess comprehension of the game from students' retelling of the story.
- Check completion of the scavenger hunt.
- Evaluate presentation of information and explanation of cyberad strategies in the short reports.

CyberPigs Comprehension Exercise

Play the game Privacy Playground: The First Adventure of the Three Little Cyber-Pigs and fill in the blanks:

1. Be careful about joining Internet clubs because companies can use clubs to find out _____

2. The three little cyberpigs did not get a _____ straw club house because _____

3. The pigs should have checked out the twig house offer more carefully before they bought the twig house because _____ _____

4. It turned out that the pigs need to pay $ _____ more to get the screws for the twig house.

5. The pigs should not give their credit card number on the Internet because _____

6. The pigs received $1,000 worth of hats, which were charged to their credit card, because _____ _____

7. Chatting is fun on the Internet, but there are _____, as in the real world, who may harm you. Never give out _____ or meet _____.

8. How many safety stars did you get? _____

Strategies of Cyberads That Target Children

1. **Banner ads:** These are the most popular, obvious, and easily recognized ads. They are flashy or sneaky (often getting you to click on them by appearing to be something else) and are usually 1 inch high and 6.5 inches wide. The text asks you to click on the ad to get information about products, often with the promise of something free. A banner ad for a Saturday morning show on Discovery Kids may look like this.

Watch Saturday Mornings
Prehistoric Planet on Discovery Kids NBC

Click Here

Kids Home Discovery Channel Fun and Games Travel Animal Planet

2. **Virtual environment:** You are invited to join teams, clubs, a world, a village, a town, or a planet, or you are asked to enter a site to play games or enter contests for grand prizes by filling in short surveys or answering a few questions in order to provide a personal profile. By doing so, you give advertisers information about what you like and dislike so that they can sell you products in the future. Advertisers also get your name, age, telephone number, mailing address, and e-mail address in this way. Here are some examples:

Example 1: A Web site may invite kids to be a part of a team with the following ad:

> Are you an outdoor adventurer, a science buff, a computer wizard, or a bookworm? Here you can find kids who are just like you. To join the crew, just punch in a few answers to the Automatic Personal Profiler and it will find the team that is just for you.

By filling in this automatic personal profiler, you end up giving out information, such as where you live, where and when you were born, number of siblings, biggest collections, how you describe yourself, your e-mail address, and so forth.

Example 2: Another Web site may invite people to join in family fun with the promise of free stuff:

Welcome to the finest site for Family Fun! You are one step away from games, contests, free e-mail, live chat, and a lot more FREE stuff. Just enter your e-mail address below! You will then be entered in the $500 gift certificate sweepstakes.

Right after you enter your e-mail address, your e-mail inbox will be flooded with messages inviting you to buy this or that.

3. ***Product spokescharacter:*** You are invited to interact with, talk to, or play with familiar characters in games and activities, such as coloring pages, crossword puzzles, and word searches featuring brand-name products and their spokescharacters. These characters are related to products or companies who want you to recognize and remember their brands so that you will buy their products.

    Example 1: You can play games such as Goblet Wordsearch, Quidditch Wordsearch, and Sorting Hat with Harry Potter on the Harry Potter Web site (http://www.harry potterfans.com/).

    Example 2: Disney's Web site (http://disney.go.com/park/homepage/today/flash/index.html) is a giant store with beloved characters helping to sell things to children, including vacation packages and Internet services.

4. ***Screensavers:*** Often a Web site offers you a free download of screensavers that feature certain product logos, slogans, and characters. By using the company's screensavers, you will recognize (and, they hope, purchase) their products.

5. ***Free e-mail account:*** Web sites offer free e-mail accounts and other free services, such as greeting cards, so that they can collect information from you and your friends. Advertisers can then solicit you with promotions through e-mails, build user profiles of people who visit the site, and sell information to other companies who will try to sell you products you don't need. Yahoo.com, MSN.com, WorldVillage.com, and many other sites offer free e-mail and greeting card services.

    Free E-mail
    Click Here
    YouName@888.com—World's best free e-mail address—Register now!

Other Commonly Used Cyberads
(A Reference for Teachers)

1. **_Rich-media ads:_** These are different from text-only banners. They are animated ads containing audio or video, and are often flashing or blinking or making weird sounds (Kaye and Medoff 2001).

2. **_Pop-up ads:_** These ads pop up on users' screens unexpectedly. _Interstitials_ and _superstitials_ are types of pop-up ads that require users to either close the window in which the ads appear or to further explore the ads (Kaye and Medoff 2001). Some pop-up ads are created to be impossible to close. Others open up one or more ads every time you close one, or include a fake close button that actually opens the full-page Web site ad.

Cyberad Scavenger Hunt

1. What Web site are you looking at? _____

2. Whom do you think the Web site is for? _____

3. What are the major cyberad strategies you find there? List examples.

   Banner ad: _____
   _____

   Invitation to join teams, groups, clubs, and so forth:
   _____
   _____

   Invitation to play games or enter contests or sweepstakes for prizes:
   _____
   _____

   E-mail service:
   _____
   _____

   Interact with favorite characters:
   _____
   _____

   Screensaver offers:
   _____
   _____

   Others:
   _____
   _____

4. Why do you think advertisers use these strategies? Explain briefly.
   _____
   _____

5. What will you do if you come across cyberads?
   _____
   _____

Cyberad Poems with Personification

Personification—giving thoughts and feelings to things that do not normally have any.

Thunderstorm

Thunderstorm vacations in rainforest
Thunderstorm brings rainy season to rainforest
Thunderstorm dreams about monkey swinging on trees
Thunderstorm remembers jumbo juicy mangos
Thunderstorm sings electric verse
Thunderstorm is the promise of life or death.

Choose something about cyberads and use personification to write a poem about it. For help, see the chart below. Choose a word from column A first, and then use words in column B or words of your own choice to describe the word from column A. Remember to write this as a poem!

Column A

Free gifts, cars, toys, games, or movies
Personal information
Free e-mail or spam
Clubhouse or team
Banner or screensaver
$1,000 prize
Disney vacation or Harry Potter
Adventures, such as travel to the moon

Column B

Feel, touch, show, is/are, yell, scream, cry, hurt
Drink, eat, taste
Move, walk, run, jump, swim, play, fly
Miss, think, remember, forget
Brainstorm, inspire, encourage, motivate
Love, like, hate, forgive
Fail, promise, scare
Drop, fall, pay, surprise, wonder, meet, call

Touring the World with Greeting Cards

Rationale

Designing and sending greeting cards to friends and relatives via electronic mail is an efficient way to communicate through the Internet. With animation and sound, Internet greeting cards are much more attractive than traditional cards and provide an excellent way to motivate students to write and to learn about other cultures and countries.

Objectives

- Students will create, send, and receive online greeting cards.
- Students will learn to use e-mail emoticons.
- Students will explore occasions or holidays celebrated by other countries and cultures.

Related Content Areas

- *Language arts:* Students will write letters and greeting cards.
- *Social studies:* Students will learn about other cultures, countries, traditions, and holidays; nurture culture awareness, tolerance, and appreciation; identify countries on a map; and name the continents of the world.
- *Math:* Students will read and understand scales on a map and estimate distances between two places.
- *Fine arts:* Students will learn how symbols communicate meanings and practice using symbols; understand music and art related to various cultures; and use art, music, and dramatic performance in a presentation.

Preparation and Materials

- Provide students with computers with Internet access and printers.
- Set up a classroom computer to use with the class as a whole. If possible, connect the computer to an overhead projector to enlarge the screen.
- Bookmark or add to the Favorites list on student computers the following sites:
  Regards.com: http://www.regards.com
  Awesome Cards.com: http://www.marlo.com
  Yahoo! Greetings: http://greetings.yahoo.com
  MSN.com Greetings: http://www.msn.egreetings.com
- Make copies for students of the E-mail Moods (page 148) and Holidays and Celebrations Around the World (page 149) handouts.
- Have available on your computer a sample online greeting card, preferably one you have received.
- Estimated time for unit: 5 hours.

Procedure

1. Ask students how often and in what ways they communicate with their friends and family. Brainstorm different ways that people can send messages and greetings to one another. Ask students to share their likes and dislikes about communicating in these ways: telephone, postal mail, e-mail, in person, and short message service (SMS) through cellular phones.
2. Show students an online greeting card you received. Explain the topic for today's lesson, then have students turn on all the computers and get ready to

go online. (Students may work in pairs or small groups, depending on how many computers you have in the classroom.)

3. Review or teach letter writing and greeting card writing formats. Pass out the E-mail Moods handout and go over it with the class.

4. Ask students to access one of the greeting card sites you bookmarked for them or added to their Favorites lists.

5. Show students how to select the type of card they wish to send and then the specific card. Everyone composes and sends a card to you by following these steps:

   - Type your e-mail address and their own e-mail addresses where the site specifies.
   - Type a subject and then a message where specified.
   - Try to use at least two emoticon symbols.
   - Click "preview card" when done and make changes as necessary.
   - When finished, e-mail the card.

6. Next have students try using another site to send greetings to a friend. Discuss which site they like the best. Ask student volunteers to share greeting cards they have received, and share the cards you have received with the class.

7. Ask students to go to the sections of the greeting card sites that have cards for different occasions. Have them look at the greetings sent on different occasions by people and work in pairs to choose special occasions that people from other cultures or countries celebrate and to send greeting cards to each other related to the occasions they chose.

8. Each pair researches one chosen occasion from another country and writes a brief report about it. The report should include information on what the celebration is about, customs and traditions behind it, and when and where the celebration occurs. Pass out the Holidays and Celebrations Around the World handout for students to use as a reference.

9. Teach or review map-reading skills, particularly to understand scale. Teach or review estimation and the continents of the world.

10. Ask students to estimate from a map, using the scale, how far their chosen countries are from where they are in the United States. Have them identify which continent the country is on.

11. To conclude and celebrate the unit, students share their reports on different holidays and occasions for which people from various countries and cultures would send greeting cards to each other. They may show the chosen culture through dress, food, music, art, or any other visual they choose.

Adaptations

- For gifted, upper elementary, and middle school students, establish e-mail pals with students in another country to learn more about each other's country. Try Epals Classroom Exchange at http://www.epals.com to find classrooms in other countries to participate in the e-mail exchange.

- For lower elementary, special needs, or ESL students, adapt steps 7 and 8 to have students write down the names of the celebrations and the countries of their origins instead of sending cards and researching a celebration.

- You may choose to teach from the handouts instead of giving them to children, depending on the age and reading level of your students.

> ➤ **TIP**
>
> *You might have class celebrations of different holidays throughout the school year, with students researching the holiday, sending greeting cards, and perhaps getting to know a penpal or e-pal from different countries that celebrate the holiday.*

Assessments

- Check whether students complete and send a card with the correct letter format and mechanical correctness.

- Observe whether students follow directions in exploring other Web sites.

- Evaluate whether students estimate the distances between their chosen countries and the United States correctly, and whether they identify the continents correctly.

- Evaluate student reports for fulfillment of all the requirements and mechanical correctness.

E-mail Moods

Talking to friends by e-mail is great because it is instant, without worries about stamps or phone bills. However, you miss your friends' facial expressions, body language, and tones of voice when talking online. Little pictures made with keyboard characters were created to help you show people how you feel in e-mails or chat rooms. To get the meaning of an emoticon (emotions and icons), turn your page 90 degrees to the right (or read sideways). You can create your own symbol and add it to this growing list.

:-)   A happy face. Someone is happy, joking, or smiling.

:-(A sad face. Someone is sad, upset, or unhappy.

:`(A sad face with tears. Someone is unhappy and crying.

:-C   Someone is really unhappy, upset, or disappointed about something.

^^^   Someone is being silly and giggling.

~:(Someone is angry.

:-@   Someone is very angry, yelling and screaming.

:-D   Someone finds something to be very funny and is laughing hard.

:-x   "OK, my lips are zipped. I promise I will not tell."

Holidays and Celebrations Around the World

Here are a few of the holidays celebrated in different countries:

Australia: New Year's Day, Australia Day, Christmas Day, and Boxing Day

Austria: Epiphany, Corpus Christi, and Immaculate Conception

Canada: Victoria Day, Canada Day, and Boxing Day

China: Lunar New Year, Dragon Boat Festival, and Mid-Autumn Festival

Finland: Maundy Thursday

France: Victory Day, Armistice Day, Bastille Day

Germany: Ascension Day, Day of Unity, and Whit Monday

Ireland: St. Patrick's Day

Italy: Epiphany, Assumption Day, Immaculate Conception, and St. Stephen's Day

Japan: Greenery Day, Respect of the Aged Day, Culture Day, and Children's Day

Luxembourg: All Saints Day, Whit Monday, and May Day

Mexico: Juarez Day, Constitution Day, and Battle of Puebla Day

New Zealand: Anazc Day and Queen's Birthday Observance

Singapore: Chinese New Year, Hari Raya Haji, Good Friday, Deepavali, and Hari Raya Puasa

South Africa: Human Rights Day, Family Day, Workers' Day, Youth Day, and Good Will Day

Thailand: Songkran Festival, Family Day, and Constitution Day

United Kingdom: St. Patrick's Day, Good Friday, Easter Monday, and Boxing Day

United States: Memorial Day, Mother's Day, Father's Day, Valentine's Day, Independence Day, Halloween, and Thanksgiving

Answer Keys for Worksheets

Unit 1

Getting to Know Mass Media

Possible answers for Questions questions 1–4:

1. TV set and CD player. Watch TV for fun and listen to music on CD. Both are electronic. TV has both live sound and pictures, and CD has sound only but can be played back at any time.
2. News report on CNN, and weather report section in newspapers.
3. Video games and movies.
4. Clips of advertising from a weekend issue of the newspaper. A picture of a billboard from the street.

Unit 2

Inventor of Television

Possible information for students to include in their stories:

Philo Taylor Farnsworth was an inventor who made possible today's TV industry, the TV shots from the moon, and satellite pictures. He was born on August 19, 1906, in a log cabin near Beaver City, Utah. He worked as a farmhand when he was young. He rode a horse to high school. He first thought of sending pictures over wires when he was 14 and working in a potato field. Philo was intrigued with the electron and electricity when he was young. He read *Popular Science* and other technical magazines and persuaded his chemistry teacher, Justin Tolman, to give him special instruction and to allow him to audit a senior course.

Farnsworth went to Brigham Young University for two years and left because of the death of his father. He did all kinds of jobs to provide for his family, including logging, repairing and delivering radios, selling electrical products door to door, and working on the railroad as an electrician. When he was 21, he got married, found investors, moved to San Francisco, and set up a laboratory. On September 7, 1927, he transmitted the first all-electronic television picture. He exclaimed, "There you are—electronic television!" when the image went through.

Farnsworth continued his research for three more years when competitions and legal disputes appeared. For the next 10 years, Farnsworth was involved in court battles with Vladimir Zworykin, who was supported by RCA, over who really invented television. In 1934, the United States Patent Office awarded Farnsworth the priority of invention. RCA had to pay one million dollars in royalties to Farnsworth.

Apart from television, Farnsworth also did research in many other areas. His other inventions included the electron microscope and the first infant incubator. He was involved in the development of radar, peacetime uses of atomic energy, and the nuclear fusion process. Farnsworth was made neither rich nor famous by his invention. He suffered from depression and other health problems later in his life. Before his death at the age of 64 in 1971, he held more than 300 U.S. and foreign patents. In 1983, the U.S. Postal Service issued a stamp bearing his portrait. In 1990, a bronze statue of Farnsworth, the "Father of Television," was placed in Statuary Hall as Utah's second honoree.

Unit 8

Violence Track Sheet Answer Key

Examples of violence found in *Tom and Jerry Kids—S.O.S. in Ninja*

1. Door hits Tom. Tom becomes flat but is unharmed.
2. Tom tries to scare Jerry with paws and roars. Jerry is not scared.
3. Tom tries to hit ninja with a spade.
4. Ninja puts spade around Tom's neck. Tom is not hurt.
5. Tom catches Jerry with a spoon.
6. Tom ties Jerry with ropes.
7. Ninja fights Tom.
8. Ninja fells flagpole. Tom falls off pole and from house.
9. Tom steals and swallows the ninja's belt.
10. Two ninjas chop down the mailbox with Tom in it. Tom comes out unharmed.
11. Many ninjas challenge Tom in a tree.

Unit 9

Programs with Reality and Fantasy Answer Key

Possible examples for each category:

Real events: Discovery Channel programs, news reports, documentaries, and National Geographic Channel programs

Actors and actresses: situation comedies, dramas, and soap operas

Real people: talk shows, game shows, interviews of celebrities, reality shows

Animation: any cartoons

Combination (shows with both animation and actors): *Barney and His Friends*

Reality-based: educational programs, how-to programs (such as on the Learning Channel and PBS)

Fantasy-based: superhero shows, Harry Potter, Peter Pan

Hero *Discussion Guide Answer Key*

Possible answers to questions 1-12:

1. His name was Ying Zheng, better know as Qin Shi Huang.

2. He lived during the Qin Dynasty (259-210 BC).

3. He was the first emperor in Chinese history. He was a ruthless but efficient ruler. He united China 2000 years ago for the first time in history and established a complete bureaucratic system during his reign (221-206 BC), meaning he set up systems for people to make policies and help run society. He standardized the money system, weighing system, and Chinese writing system. He built the Great Wall of China to defend against invasions from other countries.

4. The tomb of Qin Shi Huang is in Xian, the ancient capital city of China. His enormous tomb is still under excavation, but what have been found are astonishing both in terms of magnitude and historical importance. One of the most amazing discoveries is the 7000 terra cotta full-size soldiers buried in the tomb. They are armored, uniformed, and armed according to official military rank and order.

5. Gong Fu is a generic term for martial arts originated in China. A literal translation of the term would be "hard work" or "effort."

6. Wrestling is a sport involving throwing and grappling. Judo is also a sport that involves primarily throwing and grappling. It is very similar to wrestling and was invented in the late 1800s by Jigoro Kano, in Japan, as a sport, not for combat or self defense. Karate, a method of combat, is a power-oriented style with hard blocks and strikes and few if any throws. Tae kwon do is a Korean art similar to karate but emphasizing the feet as weapons; it is also power-oriented. Gong fu has both hard and soft styles, which describes the nature of the movements and the level of relaxation in the body; in most styles, technique and speed are more important than power. Gong fu is a broader and more complex system of combat than other styles because it teaches the use of throws, grappling, holds, weapons, and self-defense.

7. No, these actions are fantasy. They are imagined and exaggerated to make the movie fun and entertaining; they are not real. In reality, nobody, including gong fu masters, can really fly like that. The producer of the movie used

special effects to make the actors seem to fly and walk on water.

8. No. It is exaggerated and sensationalized by the movie. They cannot possibly block millions of moving iron arrows with their bodies.

9. The producer uses special effects, makeup, camera techniques, and digital effects and editing to make the impossible appear possible.

10. It is not believable. This movie romanticizes Qin. He was a tyrant ruler. According to history, Jing Ke, a man from the state of Yan, tried to assassinate him but failed. Qin slew him and revenged the attempt at his life by invading and taking the state of Yan. He even burned books and buried scholars alive who did not agree with him.

11. No. The characters are fictional.

12. Yes. I wish to see Emperor Qin let Nameless live because Nameless let him live. It is fair that way.

Unit 10

Mulan *Venn Diagram Answer Key*

Below are examples of similarities and differences between Disney's *Mulan* and the original *Ballad of Mulan*.

Disney's Mulan Story   *Similarities*   *Original Mulan Story*

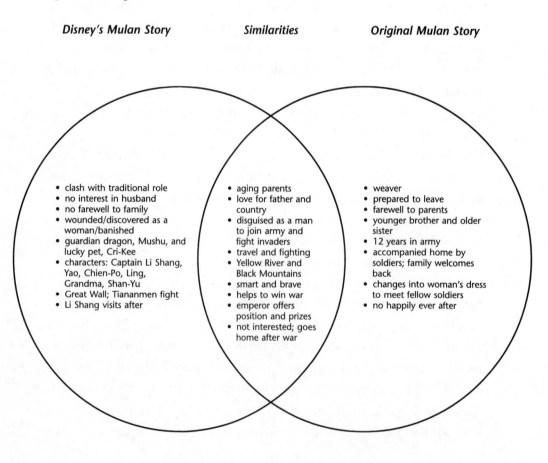

Disney's Mulan Story
- clash with traditional role
- no interest in husband
- no farewell to family
- wounded/discovered as a woman/banished
- guardian dragon, Mushu, and lucky pet, Cri-Kee
- characters: Captain Li Shang, Yao, Chien-Po, Ling, Grandma, Shan-Yu
- Great Wall; Tiananmen fight
- Li Shang visits after

Similarities
- aging parents
- love for father and country
- disguised as a man to join army and fight invaders
- travel and fighting
- Yellow River and Black Mountains
- smart and brave
- helps to win war
- emperor offers position and prizes
- not interested; goes home after war

Original Mulan Story
- weaver
- prepared to leave
- farewell to parents
- younger brother and older sister
- 12 years in army
- accompanied home by soldiers; family welcomes back
- changes into woman's dress to meet fellow soldiers
- no happily ever after

Unit 11

Viewing Guide for Home Alone Answer Key

Possible answers to questions 1-8:

1. The young boy (Kevin), villains, big brother, siblings, mother, father, uncles, and aunts

2. Villains: ugly, scary, sinister, cartoonish, clown looking, clumsy, and outwitted by kid. One is short and fat, and the other is tall and skinny.
   Kevin, the young boy: cute, naive, smarter than adults. Gets into big brother's stuff.
   Big brother: tough, mean, unsympathetic, and bully teenager.

3. Yes.
   Villains: foolish because outwitted by Kevin; clumsy (they fall all the time)
   Kevin: smart, creative, resourceful, accomplishes things beyond most kids. He fools the villains by recording movie conversations and guns shooting and scares them away. Gets into big brother's savings and buys food.
   Big brother: bully because he pushes Kevin around and threatens to hit Kevin if he touches his stuff.

4. Yes.
   Villains: dressed like clowns and criminals.
   Kevin: dressed like a cute, typical, smart, and good boy.
   Big brother: ordinary teenager dress—big shirt and pants.

5. Yes.
   Villains: clown looking. One is short and fat, and the other is tall and skinny.
   Kevin: cute, smart, and thoughtful.
   Big brother: big, tough, serious, and mean looking.

6. Yes.
   Villains: talk fast in squeaky and clownlike voices.
   Kevin: talks and reasons like a little adult.
   Big brother: uses mean voice to talk to Kevin.

7. The characters are unrealistic. They are exaggerated to entertain us.

8. Yes. They are stereotypes.

Unit 18

Dos and Don'ts of Netiquette Sample Answers

Dos

Respect other people's privacy
Be brief whenever possible.
Be patient with newbies.
Check e-mail frequently.
Be polite and courteous at all times.
Use correct grammar and spelling.
Use your best manners online.

Don'ts

Don't start flame wars.
Don't spam.
Don't pass on long chain letters.
Don't use all capital letters.
Don't use bad or rude language.
Don't break any laws.
Don't send e-mail before you calm down if you are upset.
Don't give away your password.
Don't copy other's work from online without permission.

Unit 19

Answer Key for CyberPigs Comprehension Exercise

Possible answers to questions 1-7:

1. information about you so that they can sell you things you do not need.
2. real; companies do not give something for nothing.
3. things can be made to look bigger, better, and nicer on the Internet than they actually are, and often there is a hidden price to pay.
4. $99,999.99 (Note: This is the only correct answer for this question.)
5. the Internet is a public place and you never know who will read your e-mails or the information you transmit through a website.
6. the club turns out to be a store operated by an unethical person who has the pigs' personal information.
7. strangers; never give out your address and never meet anyone in person without your parents.

Valuable Resources for Teachers

Each of the following websites is a valuable and useful resource for K-12 teachers who intend to teach media literacy in their classrooms. The websites include national and international professional associations for media literacy, listservs, sites to learn more about where media literacy fits with state learning standards, and sites for lesson plans and teaching strategies. From each site, you will find links to other useful websites that will assist you in your endeavor to teach media literacy.

Alliance for a Media Literate America: www.AMLAinfo.org/

> The AMLA is a national organization that aims to bring media literacy education to all 60 million students in the United States, their parents, their teachers, and others who care about youth. It organizes and provides national leadership, advocacy, networking, and information exchange.

Association for Media Literacy: www.aml.ca/

> The Association for Media Literacy was founded in 1978 in Canada. According to its own description, it is "made up of teachers, librarians, consultants, parents, cultural workers, and media professionals who are concerned about the impact of mass media on the creation of contemporary culture." It has members from around the world.

Center for Media Literacy: www.medialit.org

> As a pioneer in media literacy in the United States, the center provides leadership, professional development, and educational resources for media literacy education.

Children Now: www.childrennow.org

> Children Now is a research and action organization that works to improve the quality of news and entertainment media both for children and about children's issues. It also helps parents learn how to talk with their kids about tough issues like sex, AIDS, violence, drugs, and alcohol. It has research about children and families available online.

Children's Books About Unfairness, Stereotypes, Tolerance, and Activism:
northonline.sccd.ctc.edu/eceprog/anti.html

> This site lists children's books with the general theme of antibias and tolerance, compiled by Julie Rotondo Bisson. It offers short reviews for each book on the list.

Media Literacy Clearinghouse: www.med.sc.edu:1081

> This site, designed by Frank Baker, provides K-12 teachers with articles, background, and lesson plans that integrate media literacy into classroom instruction.

Media Literacy Review:
http://interact.uoregon.edu/MediaLit/mlr/home/index.html

> This is a biannual online publication, available to educators, producers, students, and parents for free. *Media Literacy Review* links visitors to active media education sites around the world and offers article databases and a directory of international organizations.

Mid-Continent Research for Education and Learning:
www.med.sc.edu:1081/mcrel.htm

> From this site, you will learn more about where and how media literacy fits in with national teaching standards.

New Mexico Media Literacy Project: www.nmmlp.org

> Established in 1993, the NMMLP has provided speakers, multimedia workshops, and videos and CD-ROMs on a variety of media literacy topics to children and adults across the nation.

Project Look Sharp's Media-L: www.ithaca.edu/looksharp/resources/
media-l.html

> This is a useful site for teachers, administrators, media professionals, and researchers who are actively involved in media literacy education. This site promotes the integration of media literacy into school curriculum at all levels. It provides strategies, advice, and resources for media literacy education.

State-by-State Media Frameworks: www.med.sc.edu:1081/statelit.htm

> This site by R. Kubey and F.W. Baker shows teachers where media literacy exists in their state standards.

Bibliography

Agassi, M. 2000. *Hands Are Not For Hitting.* Minneapolis, MN: Free Spirit Publishing.

Amit. 2002a. "How Do I Know When a Website Is Good?" http://www.acsd.k12.ca.us/tlc/library/howtouseweb.html#webeval (Accessed August 18, 2004)

Amit. 2002b. "Learn about Emoticons." http://www.amit.org.il/learning/english/netiquette/ (Accessed August 18, 2004)

Ananova. 2002. "Designing Ananova." http://www.ananova.com/about/story/sm_128668.html (Accessed August 18, 2004)

Anti-Defamation League. 2003a. "Prejudice: What to Tell Your Child About Prejudice and Discrimination." http://www.adl.org/what_to_tell/whattotell_intro.asp (Accessed August 18, 2004)

———. 2003b. Resources for Classroom and Community. http://www.adl.org/catalog/default.asp (Accessed August 18, 2004)

Armstrong, S. 1995. *Telecommunications in the Classroom.* Palo Alto, CA: Computer Learning Foundation and International Society for Technology in Education.

Ask Jeeves. 2003. Ask Jeeves Kids. http:// www.ajkids.com (Accessed August 18, 2004)

Baker, F. 2003. "Media Literacy: Yes, It Fits in Math and Science Classrooms." http://www.enc.org/focus/literacy/document.shtm?input=FOC-002081-index (Accessed August 18, 2004)

Bang, M. 2000. *When Sophie Gets Angry, Really, Really Angry.* New York, NY: Blue Sky Press.

Baran, S., and D. Davis. 2003. *Mass Communication Theory: Foundations, Ferment, and Future* (Third Ed.). Belmont, CA: Wadsworth/Thomson Learning.

Barchers, S. 1994. *Teaching Language Arts: An Integrated Approach.* New York, NY: West Publishing Company.

Barnes and Nobles and ADL. 2001. "101 Ways to Combat Prejudice." http://www.adl.org/prejudice/default.asp (Accessed August 18, 2004)

Berenstein, S., and J. Berenstein. 1984. *The Berenstein Bears and Too Much TV.* New York, NY: Random House.

Berkeley Pop Culture Project. 1991. *The Whole Pop Catalog.* Berkeley, CA: Avon Books.

Blume, J. 1972. *Tales of a Fourth Grade Nothing.* New York, NY: Random House.

———. 1980. *Superfudge.* New York, NY: Random House.

Brandenberg, A. 1990. *My Five Senses.* New York, NY: HarperCollins Publishers.

Brown, J. 2001. "Media Literacy and Critical Television Viewing in Education." In *Handbook of Children and the Media,* edited by D. G. Singer and J. Singer, 681-697. Thousand Oaks, CA: Sage Publications.

Brown, M. 1984. *Bionic Bunny Show.* Boston, MA: Atlantic Monthly Press/Little Brown and Company.

Buck, C., and K. Lima. 1999. *Tarzan.* Burbank, CA: Walt Disney Home Video.

The Cartoon Network.com. 2003. http://www.cartoonnet work.com (Accessed August 18, 2004)

The Center for Media Education. 1999. Most Popular Children's Web Sites. http://www.media-awareness.ca/english/resources/educational/ teaching_backgrounders/internet/popular_childrens_web.cfm (Accessed August 18, 2004)

Chinavoc. 2002. "People: Qin Shihuang–the First Emperor in Chinese History." http://www.chinavoc.com/history/qin/qinshh.htm (Accessed August 18, 2004)

Cole, J., and B. Degen. 1990. *The Magic School Bus Inside the Human Body.* New York, NY: Scholastic.

Columbus, C. 1990. *Home Alone.* Los Angeles, CA: 20th Century Fox Film Corporation.

Consortium of National Arts Education Associations. 1994. *National Standards for Arts Education: What Every Young American Should Know and Be Able to Do in the Arts.* Reston, VA: Music Educators National Conference.

Cook, B., and T. Bancroft. 1998. *Mulan.* Burbank, CA: Walt Disney Home Video.

Cox, C. 1996. *Teaching Language Arts.* Needham Heights, MA: Simon & Schuster.

Cullingford, C. 1984. *Children and Television.* New York, NY: St. Martin's Press.

Diaz, A. P. 1999. "Kids Use Media Nearly 40 Hours a Week." *Advertising Age,* 70 (49): 28.

DiscoveryKids.com. 2003. http://kids.discovery.com (Accessed August 18, 2004)

Disney Online. 2003. http://disney.go.com/park/homepage/today/flash/ index.html (Accessed August 18, 2004)

Dubowski, C. 1998. *Disney's Mulan: Junior Novel.* Burbank, CA: Disney Press.

Duncan, B., et al. 1989. *Media Literacy Resources Guide.* Toronto: Ontario Ministry of Education.

Fishbein, H. 1987. "Socialization and Television." In *Media, Knowledge, and Power,* edited by O. Boyd-Barrett and P. Braham, 299-318. London: The Open University.

Frank, A. 1993. *Anne Frank: The Dairy of a Young Girl.* Translated by B. M. Mooyaart. Upper Saddle River, NJ: Prentice Hall.

Gabriel, M., and E. Goldberg. 1995. *Pocahontas.* Burbank, CA: Walt Disney Home Video.

Geronimi, C. 1987. *Cinderella.* Burbank, CA: Walt Disney Home Video.

Granfield, L. 1993. *Extra! Extra! The Who, What, Where and Why of Newspapers.* Toronto, Ontario: Kids Can Press.

Gutman, D. 1996. *The Kid Who Ran for President.* New York, NY: Scholastic.

Hand, D. 1993. *Snow White and the Seven Dwarfs.* Burbank, CA: Walt Disney Home Video.

Hobbs, R. 1996. "Expanding the Concept of Literacy." In *Media Literacy in the Information Age,* edited by R. Kubey. New York: Transaction Press. http://interact.uoregon.edu/medialit/mlr/readings/articles/hobbs/expanding.html (Accessed August 18, 2004)

———. 1997. *Television Goes to School.* Manuscript in preparation.

Hoffman, M. 1991. *Amazing Grace.* Reading, MA: Scott Foresman.

Jackson. E. 1998. *Cinder Edna.* New York, NY: Mulberry Books.

Joint Committee on National Health Education Standards. 1995. *National Health Education Standards: Achieving Health Literacy.* Reston, VA: Association for the Advancement of Health Education.

Kaur, K. 2003. "SIA Plane Makes Emergency Landing at Auckland Airport." *The Straits Time* (Singapore), March 13, 2003, H7.

Kaye, B., and N. Medoff. 2001. *Just a Click Away: Advertising on the Internet.* Boston, MA: Allyn and Bacon.

Kidsdomain. 2002. "Kids Domain Safe Surfing! A Kid's Guide to Etiquette on the Net." http://www.kidsdomain.com/brain/computer/surfing/netiquette_kids.html (Accessed August 18, 2004)

Kline, S. 1989. *Herbie Jones Superhero.* New York, NY: Scholastic.

Kubey, R., and F. Baker. 1999. "Has Media Literacy Found a Curricular Foothold?" *Education Week,* 19 (October 17), 56.

Kuo, A. 2002. "The Mulan FAQ." http://www.geocities.com/Hollywood/5082/mulanfaq.html (Accessed August 18, 2004)

Loh, S. 2003. "Here to Stay, so Let's Learn to Live with It." *The Sunday Times* (Singapore), April 13, 2003, 29.

Magid, L. 1998. "Child Safety on the Information Highway." National Center for Missing and Exploited Children. http://www.safekids.com/child_safety.htm (Accessed August 18, 2004)

Marsoli, L. 1998. *Disney's Mulan: Classic Storybook.* Burbank, CA: Disney Press.

Max, J. et al. *Spider Spins a Story: Fourteen Legends from Native America.* Flagstaff, AZ: Rising Moon, Northland Publishing.

McEntee, B., G. Trousdale, and K. Wise. 1991. *Beauty and the Beast.* Burbank, CA: Walt Disney Home Video.

Media Awareness Network. 1998. "Privacy Playground: The First Adventure of the Three Little CyberPigs." http://www.media-awareness.ca/english/special_initiatives/games/privacy_playground/index.cfm (Accessed August 18, 2004)

———. 2000. "Cybersense and Nonsense: The Second Online Adventure of the Three CyberPigs." http://www.media-awareness.ca/english/special_initiatives/games/cybersense_nonsense/index.cfm (Accessed August 18, 2004)

———. 2001. "Photographic Truth in the Digital Era." http://www.media-awareness.ca/english/resources/educational/teachable_moments/photo_truth.cfm (Accessed August 18, 2004)

———. 2002a. "Online Hate: An Introduction." http://www.media-awareness.ca/english/issues/online_hate/index.cfm (Accessed August 18, 2004)

———. 2002b. "Why Teach Media Literacy?" http://www.media-awareness.ca/english/teachers/media_literacy/why_teach_media_liter.cfm (Accessed August 18, 2004)

———. 2003. "The Five Key Concepts of Media Education." http://www.media-awareness.ca/english/resources/educational/teachable_moments/5_key_concepts.cfm (Accessed August 18, 2004)

Merbreier, W. C. 1996. *Television: What's Behind What You See.* New York, NY: Farrar, Strauss and Giroux.

National Association for Sport and Physical Education. 1995. *Moving into the Future, National Standards for Physical Education: A Guide to Content and Assessment.* St. Louis: Mosby.

National Communication Association. 1998. "Competent Communicators: K-12 Speaking, Listening, and Media Literacy Standards and Competency Statements." http://www.natcom.org/Instruction/K-12/K12Stds.htm (Accessed August 18, 2004)

National Council for the Social Studies. 1994. *Expectations of Excellence: Curriculum Standards for Social Studies.* Washington, DC: Author.

National Council of Teachers of English and International Reading Association. 1996. *Standards for the English Language Arts.* Urbana, IL: NCTE; Newark, DE: IRA.

National Council of Teachers of Mathematics. 2000. *Principles and Standards for School Mathematics.* Reston, VA: Author.

National Institute on Media and the Family. 2002. "Children and the Media Violence." http://www.mediafamily.org/facts/facts_vlent.shtml (Accessed August 18, 2004)

National Press Photographers Association. 2000. "Ethics in the Age of Digital Photography." http://www.nppa.org/services/bizpract/eadp/eadp8.html (Accessed August 18, 2004)

National Research Council. 1996. *National Science Education Standards.* Washington, DC: National Academy Press.

National Standards in Foreign Language Education Project. 1996. *Standards for Foreign Language Learning: Preparing for the 21st Century.* Lawrence, KS: Author.

Naughton, K., and J. Halpert. 2001. "Hi, I'm Luxury and I'll Be Your Car." *Newsweek* E-Life Special Issue (Winter): 20-22.

New Mexico Media Literacy Project. 2003. "BadAd Contest." http://www.nmmlp.org (Accessed August 18, 2004)

The New York Times Company. 2003. "The *New York Times* on the Web: Learning Network, Grades 3-12." http://www.nytimes.com/learning/ index.html (Accessed August 18, 2004)

Ontario Ministry of Education, Intermediate and Senior Division. 1989. *Media Literacy.* Toronto: Ministry of Education.

Patience, J. 1989. *Cinderella.* New York: Price Stern Sloan.

Paterson, K. 1987. *Bridge to Terabithia.* New York, NY: HarperCollins.

Pokemon World. 2003. http://www.pokemon.com (Accessed August 18, 2004)

Polacco, P. 1996. *Aunt Chip and the Great Triple Creek Dam Affair.* New York, NY: Philomel Books.

Polland, B. 2001. *We Can Work It Out: Conflict Resolution for Children.* Berkeley, CA: Ten Speed Press/Tricycle Press.

Reitherman, W. 1987. *Aristocats.* Burbank, CA: Walt Disney Home Video.

Roberts, Russell. 2003. *Philo T. Farnsworth: The Life of Television's Forgotten Inventor.* Elkton, MD: Mitchell Lane Publishers, Inc.

Scheibe, C. 2002. "Project Look Sharp: 12 Basic Principles for Incorporating Media Literacy into any Curriculum." http://www.ithaca.edu/looksharp/resources/integration/12principles.html (Accessed August 18, 2004)

Scholastic. 2003. *Scholastic News.* http://teacher.scholastic.com/scholasticnews (Accessed August 18, 2004)

Scieszka, J. 1997. *The True Story of the 3 Little Pigs.* New York, NY: Penguin.

Semali, L., and A. Pailliotet, eds. 1999. *Intermediality.* Boulder, CO: Westview Press.

Shea, V. 1994. *Netiquette.* San Francisco, CA: Albion Books.

Shepherd, R. 1993. "Why Teach Media Literacy." *Teach Magazine*, (October/November). http://www.media-awareness.ca/english/teachers/ media_literacy/why_teach_media_liter.cfm (Accessed August 18, 2004)

Singapore Ministry of Health. "SARS Update." *The Straits Times*, April 13, 2003, H1.

Southern Poverty Law Center. 2002a. "Symbols of Hate." http://www.splcenter.org/intelligenceproject/ip-index.html (Accessed August 18, 2004)

———. 2002b. "U.S. Map of Hate Groups." http://www.tolerance.org/ maps/hate/index.html (Accessed August 18, 2004)

St. John, S. 1992. *Tom and Jerry Kids—S.O.S. in Ninja.* New York, NY: Turner Entertainment Co.

Sutton, R. 1993. "Information Literacy Meets Media Literacy and Visual Literacy." In *Art, Science and Visual Literacy: Selected Readings from the Annual Conference of the International Visual Literacy Association* (ED 363307). Pittsburgh, PA: International Visual Literacy Association.

Thoman, E. 1995. *Operational Definition of Media Literacy.* Los Angeles, CA: Center for Media Literacy.

Tripp, L. 2003. "Workshop Report: How to Do Assessment and Evaluation in Media Literacy." http://www.medialit.org/reading_room/article18.html (Accessed August 18, 2004)

TV Turnoff Network. 2003. "TV-Turnoff Week." http://www.tvturnoff.org/week.htm (Accessed August 18, 2004)

Web Wombat Pty Ltd. 2003. Online Newspapers.com. http://www.onlinenewspapers.com/ (Accessed August 18, 2004)

White, E. B. 2001.*Charlotte's Web.* New York, NY: HarperCollins.

World Village. 2003. www.worldvillage.com (Accessed August 18, 2004)

Yahooligans. 2003. http://www.yahooligans.com (Accessed August 18, 2004)

Zhang, S. 1998. *The Ballad of Mulan.* Scarborough, Ontario: Pan Asian Publications.

Zhang, Y. 2003. *Hero.* Guangdong, China: Guangdong Face Audio and Video Production.

Index

Index

About the Authors

Dr. Guofang Wan has been involved in education and media literacy education since the 1980s. She has extensive teaching experience at the precollege and college levels. She is currently an associate professor in the Department of Teacher Education, College of Education, at Ohio University. She formerly taught at Bradley University. She has published articles in academic journals and presented papers at national and international conferences on media literacy and other related areas. Dr. Wan received her Ph.D. in curriculum and instruction from Pennsylvania State University.

Dr. Hong Cheng is an associate professor in the E. W. Scripps School of Journalism, College of Communication, at Ohio University. He formerly taught at Bradley University and was a senior fellow at Nanyang Technological University in Singapore (2002-2003). He has published journal articles and book chapters on advertising and mass media. He is a former head of the International Communication Division of the Association for Education in Journalism and Mass Communication, and an associate editor of the *Asian Journal of Communication*. Dr. Cheng holds a Ph.D. in mass communications from Pennsylvania State University.